D1084024

Food on the Rails

The Food on the Go Series
as part of the Rowman & Littlefield Studies in Food and Gastronomy

General Editor: Ken Albala, Professor of History, University of the Pacific
(kalbala@pacific.edu)

Rowman & Littlefield Executive Editor: Suzanne Staszak-Silva
(sstaszak-silva@rowman.com)

The volumes in the Food on the Go series explore the fascinating ways people eat while getting from one place to another and the adaptations they make in terms of food choices, cutlery and even manners. Whether it be crossing the Atlantic in grand style on a luxury steamship, wedged into an airplane seat with a tiny tray, or driving in your car with a Big Mac in hand and soda in the cup holder, food has adapted in remarkable ways to accommodate our peripatetic habits. Eating on the go may be elegant or fast, but it differs significantly from everyday eating and these books explain why in various cultures across the globe and through history. This is the first series to systematically examine how and why mobility influences our eating habits, for better and worse.

Food on the Rails: The Golden Era of Railroad Dining, by Jeri Quinzio (2014)

Food on the Rails

The Golden Era of Railroad Dining

Jeri Quinzio

ROWMAN & LITTLEFIELD
Lanham • Boulder • New York • London

Published by Rowman & Littlefield
A wholly owned subsidiary of The Rowman & Littlefield Publishing Group, Inc.
4501 Forbes Boulevard, Suite 200, Lanham, Maryland 20706
www.rowman.com

16 Carlisle Street, London W1D 3BT, United Kingdom

British Library Cataloguing in Publication Information Available

Library of Congress Cataloging-in-Publication Data
Quinzio, Jeri.
  Food on the rails : the golden era of railroad dining / Jeri Quinzio.
      pages cm
  Includes bibliographical references and index.
  ISBN 978-1-4422-2732-3 (cloth) — ISBN 978-1-4422-2733-0 (electronic)
  1. Railroads—Dining car service—History. 2. Roadside restaurants—History.
  I. Title.
  TF668.Q56 2014
  385'.22—dc23   2014010035

∞™ The paper used in this publication meets the minimum requirements of
American National Standard for Information Sciences—Permanence of Paper for
Printed Library Materials, ANSI/NISO Z39.48-1992.

Printed in the United States of America

To my mother,
Mary Mahoney Quinzio,
who always saw possibilities.

Contents

Food on the Go, Series Foreword

How familiar is the lament? "No one sits down to eat any more! People just grab something on the street or at the drive through. That's not a proper meal, it's just noshing on the way from one place to another." Food on the move is nothing new. There has always been street food and fast food. People have always eaten in transit. Our tendency to dismiss such meals as quick and convenient but never of any real gastronomic distinction does injustice to the wide variety of foods available to people traveling, and sometimes these meals could be quite elegant indeed. Think of the great caravans trekking across the steppes of Western Asia, parking their camels and setting up tents for a sumptuous feast of dried fruits, nuts, flatbreads, and freshly roasted kebabs. Or think of the great age of early air travel when airlines had their own specially designed dishware and served elegant, if seat-tray-sized, meals prepared by trained chefs. Meals served on trains in the nineteenth century were among the most celebrated of their day and of course luxury cruises pride themselves on fine dining as an indispensable feature of the entire experience. Food truck fare, offered to pedestrians, has now become the cutting edge in hip cuisine.

Traveling food need not be grand though. Sometimes it merely supplies sustenance—the hikers' trail mix or high protein pemmican to sustain the intrepid hunter on the great plains. It can also be pretty rough if we think of the war time C rations or hard tack and rum given to sailors in the colonial era. It seems as if some modes of transport have their own repertoire of foods, without which the trip would not be complete. What's a road trip without chips and junk food? Is there anyone who doesn't miss the little packs of salty peanuts on domestic flights? Traveling food also poses its own unique set of challenges, both for food preparation and consumption. Imagine stoking a fire on a wooden ship! Or flipping an omelet while the train rumbles violently over the tracks. Handheld food, perhaps the way of the future, is the quintessential traveling format, but so too are special Styrofoam containers and sporks, not to mention the leather bota, aluminum canteen, or plastic water bottle. Traveling food has its own etiquette as well, looser than the dining table, but interestingly quite private, perhaps intentionally in considering the public setting.

When I first thought of this series, I don't think I had ever thought through how many foods are specially designed for travel, or how complex and very culturally bound food eaten on trains, planes, cars, bikes, horseback can be. I will never forget a long train ride I took from Rome to the Tyrolean Alps. A young family sat across from me and they were well stocked with goods. Out came a salami, a loaf of bread, a hunk of cheese, a bottle of wine. They were making a mess, gesticulating wildly, chattering in Italian. It all looked delicious, and they savored every morsel. By the time we approached the German-speaking region, they had neatened themselves up, tidied the area, switched languages, and every trace of their Italian repast was gone, and would have been completely unseemly, I think, that far north. That is, people do have explicit gastronomic traditions for travel that are as bound up with nationhood, class, gender, and self as any other eating habit. So it is about time we thought of these kinds of meals as a separate genre, and this series I hope will fill the gap in our understanding of why we eat what we do on the move.

Ken Albala
University of the Pacific

Acknowledgments

No one writes a book alone.

Friends and acquaintances clip relevant news items, recommend books, and tell their stories about the subject at hand. Their ideas often lead to new lines of inquiry, correct misconceptions, and make the work better than it otherwise would have been. It's likely that many of them don't know they've contributed to the book. They may have made a passing remark and then forgotten it. But that remark may have led to new avenues of thought and made a major difference to the writer.

Others play a more direct role, providing photographs and recipes, reading rough drafts, correcting errors, suggesting changes. Even when we disagree, the criticism is helpful and, ultimately, appreciated.

The godmother of this book is Kyri Claflin, who recommended the project to me. Kyri's wisdom, encouragement, and support have been a source of strength for me for years. I owe her special thanks.

Series editor Ken Albala's boundless enthusiasm for food, history, and life makes working with him a joy.

Br. Thomas Ryan's extensive knowledge of trains kept me on track and helped me avoid many a derailment. I am in his debt and in Pat Kelly's for introducing us.

Thanks to Roz Cummins for remembering her mother's Pullman toy and her friend Charlotte Holt for photographing it for me. Others who generously provided photographs include Paul Smith, company archivist for Thomas Cook

UK & Ireland; Carine Corcia, of Le Train Bleu in Paris; Phoebe Janzen, Florence Historical Society and Harvey House Museum; Joann Schwendemann, Dover Books; Anne M. Baker and Shannon Mawhiney, Missouri State University; Stacey Bollinger, Strasburg Rail Road; Amanda Caskey, Venice Simplon Orient-Express; and Kyri Claflin.

Linda Stradley, Patricia Kelly, Jill O'Connor, and Erika Paggett, of the California Raisin Marketing Board, all kindly provided recipes.

I owe much to Marylène Altieri, Paula Becker, Daniel Bourque, Joe Carlin, Dan Coleman, Patricia Flaherty, Marc Frattasio, Patricia Bixler Reber, Lynn Schweikart, Nancy Stutzman, and Barbara Ketcham Wheaton for all sorts of contributions to the effort.

As always, I couldn't do this without the help of the members of my writers' workshop: Myrna Kaye, Roberta Leviton, Barbara Mende, Shirley Moskow, and Rose Yesu.

Finally, I want to thank Rowman & Littlefield editor Suzanne Staszak-Silva and assistant editor Kathryn Knigge, for their invaluable help.

Introduction

In the 1820s, when the English developed the first steam locomotive and the era of passenger rail transportation began, the world changed. For the first time, people could move faster than horses could carry them. Trips that once took weeks now took days. Those that once lasted for days were completed in hours. In the years to come, railroads would transform not only travel, but also business, communications, food distribution, dining, and social mores.

Initially, though, traveling by train was challenging. At best, it was uncomfortable. There was little or nothing to eat on early train trips, and there were no lavatories. In some places, train travel was actually dangerous. Poorly laid tracks resulted in derailments. People, animals, and tree limbs on the tracks led to train wrecks. Flying sparks from the engine ignited fires. The lack of coordination among time zones wreaked havoc with schedules and caused accidents.

The builders of railroads were not thinking about travelers' comfort, food, or even safety when they began. They were thinking about engines and track gauges. They planned to haul freight, not passengers; and freight doesn't need to be fed or provided with comfortable seats. Nor does it complain.

Despite all the difficulties, when passenger service began most people were amazed and pleased by the speed and convenience of the railways. They saw exciting possibilities through the smoke and soot. However, as with any new technology, the enthusiasm was not universal. Pope Gregory XVI (1831–1846) was opposed to railways, considering them the work of the devil. He told a French visitor that they were not "chemins de ferre," they were "chemins d'enfer," not the iron road, or railroad, but the road to hell.[1]

A less fiery, but more common, opinion was that it was difficult to make the psychological transition from, say, the city to the countryside when the trip took so much less time. Others complained that the train went too fast to allow them to appreciate the passing scenery. The French critic and author Jules Janin wrote in 1843 that he'd never take the train to Versailles again since, "You are no sooner started than you arrive! Pshaw! What is the use of setting out, unless it is to feel yourself go?" [2]

Initially trips were short, so the lack of food was not a problem. But as new routes covered longer distances, it became an issue. One of the solutions rail companies tried was providing refreshment rooms at rail stations. Steam locomotives had to stop every hundred miles or so to take on water, so this seemed sensible. Some railroads ran their own refreshment rooms; other rooms were run privately. They varied widely, but most of them sold poor quality food and few allowed passengers enough time to eat. However, because railroads developed differently in different countries and even in parts of the same country, travelers' actual experiences both on the trains themselves and in the station refreshment rooms varied greatly during the same general time frame.

In 1843, a woman living in London might have described her first railway experience this way:

This year, my husband and I took our first train trip. Two years ago, when we went to Birmingham to visit my sister and her husband, we traveled by stage-coach. The journey took nearly twelve hours, twelve long, bumpy hours to tell the truth. So we decided to take a chance on the railway. The conductor said the distance was about 112 miles and it took us just six hours. Imagine.

Twenty-two miles an hour is very fast, to be sure, but our railroads are very well built. Still, I worried about the speed until last year, when the Queen herself took a train to Scotland. If it was safe enough for Queen Victoria, I decided it was safe enough for us. Prince Albert had taken a train before, but it was the Queen's trip that finally convinced us to try it.

Of course, we didn't travel in the Queen's lovely carriage with its padded silk walls, but we bought first-class tickets. I'm told second-class cars have only wooden benches for seats.

I shouldn't wonder if the Queen had dinner in her carriage. There was no such thing on our train, but we did stop at the Wolverton Station buffet for refreshments. We were allowed only ten minutes, but that was time enough for tea and a Banbury cake. They had pork pies as well, but they looked stale, so we just had the cakes.

We left London from Euston Station, which looks just like a Greek temple. The departure hall takes my breath away. The train left at eight o'clock in the morning, and we arrived at Birmingham at two in the afternoon, in time for dinner with Sarah and Roger. I'm sure the Queen herself couldn't have had a more enjoyable trip.

A banker living in Boston in the 1850s might have offered this report on a business trip to New York:

My travel to New York is much more manageable now that nearly the entire route is aboard a train, rather than the train and steamboat arrangement of the past. Admittedly the Boston and New York Express Line is actually four different lines—the Boston and Worcester to Worcester, then the Western Railroad of Massachusetts to Springfield, then the Hartford and New Haven to New Haven, and finally the New York and New Haven to New York. When we arrived in New York, we transferred to a horse-drawn carriage to go to our hotels as the train is not allowed in the heart of the city. The trip of about 236 miles took nine hours.

Aboard the train, I tried to make myself comfortable but was disconcerted by the filth of the floor upon which I would have placed my carpetbag. I had to hold it in my lap for the duration. They should forbid tobacco chewing on trains, in my opinion.

Since I knew that nourishment would be lacking during the trip, I had an early dinner at home before we departed at half past two. There is no food served on the trains unless one counts the lads who pass through the carriages selling oranges, candies, and newspapers. Some of these news butchers, as they're called, are annoying urchins who are quick to make intentional mistakes with your change. I concede, though, that I've met a few enterprising and honest lads. Their wares are welcome enough when there's nothing else available.

As is usual we stopped at Springfield for twenty minutes to purchase a light supper. The passengers all rushed from the train to the refreshment room and with all the crowding and jostling, I was able to obtain only a hard-boiled egg.

I was grateful to get to New York and the St. Nicholas Hotel in time for a late supper and a brandy. This new establishment is equal, if not superior, to the Astor. The next day, my dinner of venison was excellent, and the claret we drank with it was superb. I plan to take Lily to the St. Nicholas soon, but I will make sure the train has a separate carriage for ladies and their escorts so she will not experience the tobacco problem.

A prospective settler riding on the Santa Fe Railroad in 1872 might have given this account of his trip:

Train travel in the West is an adventure. I felt that I had left civilization in the East and entered a raw and primitive land. Train delays and derailments are so common as to pass nearly unnoticed. We hit a cow that had been napping on the tracks and it took some time to clear up the bloody mess and proceed. The train crew took this in stride, since it happens frequently. Train robberies are not uncommon either, but fortunately I did not have that experience.

Sleep on the train was impossible, the seats being so uncomfortable. Also we had to be alert for sparks flying into the carriage because it was too warm to keep the windows closed. In any case, the smells that hang in the air make open windows necessary even in the worst weather. It is a wonder that more trains don't burn up since the locomotive throws out wild showers of fire all along the way.

I had taken some food with me, but when that was finished I had to rely on the eating houses along the line. These are hard to describe to anyone in the East. Some are little more than shacks thrown up near the rail and covered with buffalo hides to keep out the wind. Filth is taken for granted. At one place near Dodge City, buffalo meat was piled up outside, and we had to cut off a steak and take it in to the cook to be fried. The beans looked to have been heated and reheated many times over, and the coffee defied drinking. The whiskey, though not of good quality, was more tolerable.

So little time was allowed for meals that we often had barely begun to eat when the whistle blew and we had to run for the train. Some of my fellow passengers believe that the eating houses and the conductors are in league with each other to make sure there's not enough time to eat the food, so it can be sold again to the next trainload of victims. I don't know if I believe that, but anything seems possible here. This part of the country is not for the faint of heart. But there is opportunity aplenty here for those with vision. And a strong stomach.

It would be years before railroads offered their passengers relative safety, much less such amenities as comfortable seating, dining cars, and sleepers for long trips. When George M. Pullman introduced the dining car in 1867, it was widely acclaimed, but far from universally adopted. In fact, despite passenger demand, some railroad companies resisted adding the cars for years because of the expense involved.

By the turn of the twentieth century, railroad travel became almost universally safe and pleasant. In fact, for prosperous travelers it was the height of pampered luxury. Railroad cars were beautifully designed and furnished. Dining cars served meals that were considered as good as, if not better than, those served in fine dining restaurants or in grand hotels. No longer an adventure or a test of courage, railroad travel in most countries had become a safe, dependable, and often magnificent way to travel.

If only the intrepid passengers who had braved the flying soot, tobacco juice covered floors, and rickety rails of the earliest trains could have ridden the luxurious railroads of the golden era.

⌒◦ Banbury Cakes and Tarts

Banbury cakes or tarts were sold at English rail station refreshment rooms and named for the town of Banbury, in Oxfordshire, England. Banbury will sound familiar, even to Americans, because of the nursery rhyme that begins, "Ride a cock horse to Banbury Cross." According to the *Oxford English Dictionary*, the town was "formerly noted for the number and zeal of its Puritan inhabitants" and is still notable for its cakes.

An early recipe for Banbury cakes appears in Gervase Markham's 1615 *The English Housewife*. His recipe, below, mixes currants into a dough to make one cake.

To Make Banbury Cakes

To make a very good Banbury Cake, take four pounds of Currants and wash and pick them very clean, and dry them in a cloth: then take three Eggs, and put away one yelk, and beat them and strain them with the Barm, putting thereto Cloves, Mace, Cinamon, and Nutmegs, then take a pint of Cream, and as much mornings Milk, and set it on the fire till the cold be taken away; then take flowre, and put in good store of cold butter and sugar, then put in your eggs, barm and meal, and work them all together an hour or more; then save a part of the past, & the rest break in pieces, and work in your Currants, which done, mould your Cakes of what quantity you please, and then with that paste which hath not any Currants, cover it very thin, both underneath and aloft. And so bake it according to the bigness.

Later recipes generally resemble individual turnovers or tarts rather than cakes. The Banbury cakes served at English railway stations were generally derided as being old and stale, but freshly made ones are delectable. This recipe is taken, with her permission, from Linda Stradley's wonderful "What's Cooking America" website: whatscookingamerica.net. 🚃

✷ Banbury Tea Tarts

Yields: serves many
Prep time: 15 min
Bake time: 20 min

½ cup butter, room temperature
1½ cups granulated sugar
3 eggs
1 cup dried currants
Zest of 1 lemon
Juice of 1 lemon
Pastry for 9-inch one-crust pie

Preheat oven to 375 degrees F.

In a large bowl, cream the butter and sugar together thoroughly. Add eggs, currants, lemon zest, and lemon juice, stirring to mix well; set aside.

Prepare pie pastry. Roll out the pastry dough ⅛-inch thick. Tarts may be made any size. For conventional muffin pans, cut out circles with a tuna can which has both ends cut off. For miniature muffin pans, use a tomato paste can to cut out the rounds. Place pastry in the muffin pans, smoothing the dough so it has no bumps.

Stir the filling mixture. Using a teaspoon, fill the tarts ⅔ full. NOTE: Don't let the filling spill onto the pan, as it will make the tarts hard to remove.

Bake the miniature tarts approximately 15 to 20 minutes or until the pastry is a light brown. Remove from oven, remove from the muffin pans, and let cool on a wire rack.

NOTE: Because these tarts are so easy to make, I usually double the recipe and make about 9 dozen tiny tarts. They freeze beautifully, between plastic wrap. These Banbury Tea Tarts are at their best when served slightly warmed, either in a microwave or regular oven.
—Linda Stradley

CHAPTER 1

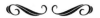

Dining before the Dining Car

The English were railroad pioneers, and their railway system was known for the high quality of its construction. In fact, the Americans and the French subsequently used English railroad technology as their model. Attention to quality and detail did not slow the development of the British rail system. In 1843, 1,800 miles of railroad were open to traffic, and the trains carried 300,000 passengers a week.[1] By 1899, 20,000 miles had opened, and passengers numbered close to 12,000,000. However, the quality of the first trains did not extend to food service or passengers' comfort. There were few amenities and little or nothing to eat onboard trains before the introduction of dining cars in the 1870s.

Some passengers packed lunch baskets to sustain themselves during trips. Those who hadn't brought anything simply grumbled about the lack of food. As more rail lines were laid and trips grew longer, the British built a series of rail station refreshment rooms and railway hotels to provide food and accommodations for their passengers. The refreshment rooms, also known as tearooms, offered simple meals and snacks—tea, soup, sandwiches, pork pies, Banbury cakes, and sausage rolls.

Sir William Acworth was a British railway economist whose career spanned the late nineteenth and early twentieth centuries. He authored several books and studies on railway economics in the British Isles, Germany, India, and the United States. Although his primary focus was on the business and politics of railways, he had strong opinions about the food that was

1

available to railway travelers. Acworth believed there was much room for improvement in the English refreshment rooms. In his 1899 book, *The Railways of England*, he wrote, "I travelled backwards and forwards across Lincolnshire for a long summer's day, some time back, and for twelve mortal hours had to batten on buns." However, he acknowledged that the refreshments were better than they'd been in the days when "the tea and the soup at Mugby Junction rested substantially on the same foundation."[2]

Charles Dickens had much the same opinion of the refreshments. He described the coffee as "brown hot water thickened with flour," and the pork pie as "glutinous lumps of gristle and grease."[3] Anthony Trollope was even more derisive. He said the real disgrace of England was the railway's "fossil sandwiches": "That whited sepulchre, fair enough outside, but so meagre, poor, and spiritless within, such a thing of shreds and parings, such a dab of food, telling us that the poor bone whence it was scraped had been made utterly bare before it was sent into the kitchen for the soup pot."[4]

The railway sandwich's freshness, or lack thereof, was ridiculed for years and often was used as a metaphor for mediocrity. It was still being joked about in David Lean's classic film *Brief Encounter*, which was set in a 1938 station refreshment room. The characters played by Trevor Howard and Celia Johnson meet and fall in love as they wait for their trains and sip their tea. In the course of the film, a rude customer says to the waitress, "If them sandwiches were made this morning, you're Shirley Temple." The "Milford Junction" of the film was actually Carnforth Station, which still exists and has been restored to look the way it did in the late 1930s. Fans of the film are among its most faithful patrons.

English refreshment stops were brief, sometimes just ten minutes. Passengers complained that they were often so rushed that the train's departure bell rang before their coffee, tea, or soup had cooled enough to sip. English writer Chris de Winter Hebron reported that once, due to a delay in a train's departure, passengers at a station actually saw their abandoned refreshments being dumped back into the urns and pots they had just been poured from, to be resold when the next train arrived.[5]

The British instituted the station refreshment room system on railways in India in the mid-nineteenth century. Acworth quoted an article in an unidentified Australian newspaper that said Indian refreshment rooms were better than those in England. Dinner at the rooms on the line from Calcutta to Bombay, according to the article, consisted of "soup and fish, beef, mutton, snipe, duck, partridge, quail, pastry, four or five different kinds of fruits, and the universal curry and rice. . . . there was a native servant to every two passengers who partook of meals."[6]

The Australian writer was dismissive of the "universal curry and rice" of India, but, years later, author David Burton took the opposite point of view in his book, *The Raj at Table*, writing that

> every big station had three dining rooms on the platform—European, Hindu and Muslim. Anybody with any sense avoided the European one, except perhaps to buy a luke-warm soda or beer, for the food was as horrendous as it was over-priced. The Muslim dining rooms were quite a different story, however, and the delicious aromas of kababs and the pilaus which wafted from them provided a temptation to many a European traveller, provided they could turn a blind eye to the kitchen conditions out the back.[7]

The Era of Travel

With the advent of industrialization in the nineteenth century, people of means began to travel more often. Not only were they becoming acquainted with different regions of their own countries, but they were also traveling to other countries. Before long, even middle- and working-class people were able to travel. In 1841, Thomas Cook persuaded a railroad company in England to run a special excursion train to a temperance meeting. Because Cook was able to guarantee a large group of passengers, the railroad company reduced its fares. The first excursion was so successful that Cook went on to organize other trips and tours, primarily for middle-class customers. Cook's Tours, as they became known, also enabled women to travel without fear. By 1863, he had conducted 2,000 visitors to France and 500 to Switzerland, arranging appropriate accommodations and food for the "roast-beef-and-pudding-eating Englishman."[8] In 1871, he established Thomas Cook & Son, which became a worldwide travel agency.

The increase in tourism travel led to the era of the grand hotel, and the English railroad companies built some of the grandest. The terminus hotels, as they were also known, were often designed by the leading architects of the day and were the most impressive buildings in their respective cities. The palaces of their time, they boasted 200–300 rooms, and included guestrooms, restaurants, meeting rooms, bars, and ballrooms along with such modern features as indoor plumbing and elevators. With enough advance planning and some luck, travelers could skip stale railway sandwiches and arrive at a terminus hotel in time for a fine dinner.

Wittingly or not, the hotels also promoted gender equality since their dining rooms were seen as respectable places for genteel ladies to dine publicly. Previously, ladies were relegated to the private dining rooms at hotels.

Thomas Cook's first European travel brochure, 1865. Courtesy of the Thomas Cook Archives

Well-to-do men also dined at their clubs, where women were not welcome. But with the advent of railway hotels, ladies were welcomed in the public dining rooms. Dining at the hotels was not only seemly, it was fashionable; it was an opportunity to dress for dinner in a style befitting the opulent surroundings.

Canadian railways followed the English example and built elaborate railway hotels, from the Banff Springs Hotel in the West to the Chateau Frontenac in Quebec. France began erecting grand hotels associated with its railways at the end of the nineteenth century, as did Germany, Italy, Belgium, and other European countries.

The French also built rail station restaurants; but in contrast to the English ones, many of them were splendid. Despite the plainness of its original name, the Buffet de la Gare de Lyon is a prime example of the lavish Belle Époque style. Every inch of its interior surface is gilded, painted, mirrored, or muraled in sumptuous splendor. Built to cater to visitors to the 1900

Cook's Tour participants at Pompeii, Italy, in 1868. Courtesy of the Thomas Cook Archives

Universal Exposition, in 1963 it was renamed Le Train Bleu after the famous train line of the same name. It has been the setting for scenes in such films as Luc Besson's *Nikita* and George Cukor's *Travels with My Aunt*, and has become a destination restaurant rather than a mere station buffet. Today, its menu includes such time-honored classics as duck foie gras, fillet of turbot, and baba au rhum as well as dishes Escoffier would not recognize like gazpacho, avocado tartare with coriander, and salmon served with a coconut emulsion and red curry.

Rapid U.S. Railway Travel

British railways were associated with quality. In the United States, speed took precedence over any other consideration, including safety. Travelers to the country often commented on the American devotion to haste, whether in laying tracks, in eating, or in daily life. The faster, the better seemed to be the American motto. In 1833, the French government sent Michel Chevalier to the United States to assess the construction of canals and railroads. He reported that, unlike in France where there was more talk of railroads than construction of them, in the United States the work was being done *à l'américaine*, meaning rapidly.[9]

Le Train Bleu at the Gare de Lyon, Paris. One of the world's most impressive rail station restaurants. Courtesy of Le Train Bleu

"Progress crawls in Europe, but gallops in America," was the way Scottish poet and journalist Charles MacKay, who toured the United States in the mid-nineteenth century and worked as a New York correspondent for the *Times*, expressed it.[10]

Frederick Marryat, a British naval officer and author, spent 1837 and 1838 traveling in Canada and the United States. He published his observations in *A Diary in America, with Remarks on Its Institutions* in 1839. In the book, he called Americans "a restless, locomotive people: whether for business or pleasure, they are ever on the move in their own country, and they move in masses." Marryat believed that American railroads were not as well made as English ones, and as a result were more dangerous, more prone to accidents. But he noted the "great object is to obtain quick returns for the outlay, and, except in few instances, durability or permanency is not thought of."[11]

American train depots were originally built to store cargo and possibly provide space where passengers could wait for trains. Some depots included basic housing for the stationmaster and his family. The stations were not designed to be restaurants. However if a stationmaster's wife was enterprising, she might set up tables on station platforms and serve homemade food to passengers when the train stopped. Depending on the cook's specialties, passengers might enjoy anything from pot roasts to freshly baked pies or biscuits. Conversely, travelers might alight at a station offering terrible food or none at all.

By the mid-nineteenth century, refreshment rooms had opened at some depots. However, even if the food was good, the time allotted for meals was inadequate. Like so many others, Marryat was struck by the speed with which Americans ate. He described the scene when trains stopped at a railroad station refreshment room:

> All the doors are thrown open, and out rush the passengers like boys out of school and crowd round the tables to solace themselves with pies, patties, cakes, hard-boiled eggs, ham custards, and a variety of railroad luxuries, too numerous to mention. The bell rings for departure, in they all hurry with their hands and mouths full, and off they go again, until the next stopping place induces them to relieve the monotony of the journey by masticating without being hungry.[12]

Judging from contemporary reports, although there might have been numerous "railroad luxuries" as Marryat said, the food was seldom good.

On June 10, 1857, *The New York Times* offered its candid opinion:

> If there is any word in the English language more shamefully misused than another, it is the word refreshment, as applied to the hurry scurry of eating and drinking at railroad stations. The dreary places . . . are called Refreshment Saloons, but there could not be a more inappropriate designation for such abominations of desolation. . . . It is expected that three or four hundred men, women and children . . . can be whirled half a day over a dusty road, with hot cinders flying in the faces; and then, when they approach a station dying with weariness, hunger and thirst, longing for an opportunity to bathe their faces at least before partaking of their much needed refreshments, that they shall rush out helter-skelter into a dismal, long room and dispatch a supper, breakfast or dinner in fifteen minutes.

The article went on to refer to this as "savage and unnatural feeding." It referred to "tough beefsteak soaked in bad butter," "stale bread," and "the inevitable custard pie," and said such foods "laid the foundation for a fit of dyspepsia, which may lead to a disease of the lungs or a fever." *The New York Times* suggested that the railroad companies should manage the eating establishments rather than leaving them in the hands of "grasping and ignorant men" who have passengers at their mercy.[13]

The New York Times was certainly not alone in its opinions. Words and phrases like "dried-up sandwiches," "fossil buns,"[14] "dry chops," "gutta-percha [a rubbery substance] steaks," and pie that "means a nightmare for a week,"[15] abound in contemporary writing.

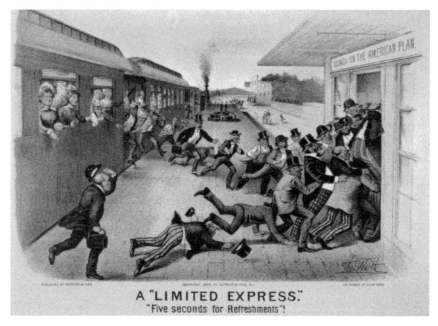

A "LIMITED EXPRESS."
"Five seconds for Refreshments"!

Currier & Ives lampooned the speed of American rail station dining in this 1884 image. Courtesy of the Library of Congress

Eating hastily was not limited to railroad station meals. Even when stopping at a hotel where there was less need for speed, Americans still ate as though time was running out. Chevalier wrote:

> In the hotels and on board the steamboats, the door of the dining hall is crowded at the approach of a mealtime. As soon as the bell sounds, there is a general rush into the room and in less than ten minutes every place is occupied. In a quarter of an hour, out of three hundred persons, two hundred have left the table, and in ten minutes more not an individual is to be seen.[16]

Like the Europeans, the Americans built grand hotels in the nineteenth century, although generally they were not constructed or run by railway companies. The meals served in their elegant dining rooms were as opulent as their surroundings. Passengers on the East Coast knew to arrange their trips so that they'd arrive in New York in time for dinner at a fine hotel such as the Astor House where they could enjoy anything from poitrine de veau au blanc to macaroni au parmesan to mince pie. They could dine in similar style at the Palmer House in Chicago or at the Tremont House in Boston. But outside the major cities, railroad passengers were unlikely to dine well or even adequately. Marryat praised Virginia's fried chicken, but noted that in the West passengers had to subsist on "*corn bread and common doings*' (i.e., bread made of Indian meal, and pork fat)."[17]

On some lines, passengers could order a lunch basket from the train attendant who would telegraph the order ahead, pick it up at a station, and serve it in the car. In the late 1800s, N & G Ohmer's Railroad Basket Lunch Service in Lafayette, Indiana, offered a selection of lunch baskets. Noting that the train did not stop for dinner, the menu listed meals such as half-dozen fried oysters, two slices of bread with butter, a piece of pie, and pickles for fifty cents; cold sugar-cured ham, two boiled eggs, two slices of bread with butter, and half-dozen olives for forty-five cents; and sardines and lemon, two slices of bread and butter, and a piece of pie for forty-five cents. The least expensive lunch consisted of pickled pig's feet, two baker's rolls with butter, pickles, and pie for thirty-five cents. Passengers could also order sandwiches, fruit, beer, wine, milk, coffee, and tea. Most of those items were ten cents, but "Claret Wine" cost seventy-five cents.[18]

Many passengers packed their own picnic lunches at home and took them to eat aboard the train. In 1915, a reporter for the *Kansas City Star* said they were called shoe box lunches and typically consisted of fried chicken, hard-boiled eggs, and some cake. But on long trips, the amount of food that passengers could take on the train was apt to run out before they reached their destination. Also, particularly in summer months, passengers complained about the smell of food brought onboard. In the same article, the writer wittily reported, "The bouquet from those lunches hung around the car all day and the flies wired ahead for their friends to meet them at each station."[19]

Some trains provided free water service for their passengers. A server would pass through the train with a tin canister filled with iced water and offer passengers a drink. Although a glass of water would be welcome, especially in warm weather, the server carried only one or two tumblers from which everyone drank. There was no provision for washing the tumblers.[20]

The News Butcher

There was another option for food aboard trains in America, although no one would call it dining. Boys called *news butchers* peddled candy, oranges, and other snacks onboard trains and at stations. In the nineteenth century, the word *butcher* was not merely associated with meat markets and mass murderers; it was also used for vendors in general. News butchers were employed by the railroads to sell newspapers, books, and snacks to passengers. The butchers were usually boys in their early teens who lacked other options to earn money and loved the chance to travel away from home, even if it was a short distance. Although they seldom earned much money, they took pride in wearing the cap that identified them as railroad employees and were thrilled when the train's engineer allowed them to ride in the engine.

Despite the convenience of the items offered by the butchers, passengers were more apt to criticize than to praise them. They said the boys sold stale sandwiches, rotten fruit, and day-old newspapers. They complained about the boys' honesty, saying they often intentionally short-changed customers. In Noel Coward's play, *Quadrille*, an American railroad tycoon tells an English lady that he went to work as a news butcher when he was thirteen. When she asks what a news butcher is, he says, "A cheeky, shrill-voiced little boy who prances through the rolling trains selling newspapers and questionable magazines and peanuts and chewing-tobacco."[21]

Robert Louis Stevenson appreciated the newsboys. In his account of his 1879 train trip from New York to San Francisco, *Across the Plains*, he recalled that a good deal of a passenger's comfort depended on the newsboys. Stevenson valued the food and services they provided since he was traveling aboard an emigrant train with few amenities. Emigrant trains offered inexpensive, but basic, transportation to those relocating west to seek their fortunes, or at least a better way of life. The newsboy, Stevenson wrote, "has it in his power indefinitely to better and brighten the emigrant's lot." Stevenson admitted that one of the newsboys he met was a "dark, bullying, contemptuous, insolent scoundrel, who treated us like dogs." But he said that another made himself the friend of all, told the passengers where and when to have meals, made sure they weren't left behind at train stops along the way, and generally looked after them. He, Stevenson said, was "a hero of the old Greek stamp . . . doing a man's work and bettering the world."[22]

Some others felt sorry for the boys, noting that customers sometimes cheated the boys by stealing soda bottles or grabbing a newspaper without paying for it. Because they had to reimburse their employers for lost or stolen merchandise, the boys might work long hours for little pay. They worked on commission; so on a good day, a news butcher might take home a few dollars. On a bad day, he could even lose money.

It is not surprising that Horatio Alger was on the side of the boys. In his story titled "The Erie Train Boy," Alger noted that the boys had to pay a deposit on their stock before they began working on the trains, a deposit they could ill afford as most were poor. Typically, Alger's young hero was supporting a widowed mother and, predictably, he became a success in life.

Like Alger's hero, some news butchers did go on to fame and fortune. Thomas Alva Edison went to work as a news butcher on the Chicago,

Detroit, and Canada Grand Trunk Junction Railroad Company in 1859 when he was just twelve years old. Like the other butchers, he sold snacks. Unlike anyone else, Edison set up a printing press on the train and produced the first newspaper published on a moving train. He called it the *Grand Trunk Herald*. He charged a penny an issue, eight cents for a monthly subscription. He also stored equipment for his chemistry experiments on the train, and one day an experiment started a fire in the baggage car. The conductor was so upset he relegated Edison to working at the station. Today there is a Thomas Edison Depot museum located at the Port Huron, Michigan, depot where he peddled his wares.

Thomas Edison's chemistry experiments were not appreciated by the railroad. Courtesy of the Bridgeman Art Library

Walt Disney and his older brother Roy both worked as news butchers when teenagers. Roy worked on the Santa Fe Railroad for two summers. A few years later, in 1917, Walt went to work for the Van Noy Interstate Company on railroad lines that ran between Kansas City and Chicago.

Sixteen years old when he was hired, Walt Disney didn't fare well as a news butcher. His coworkers played practical jokes on him and customers took advantage of his inexperience to cheat him. He couldn't resist sampling the candy he was supposed to sell, so he often ended up owing more than he earned. Nevertheless, he loved traveling on the rails and became a lifelong railroad buff. After he achieved success, he had a one-eighth-scale railroad built on his California estate. He featured railroads in his theme parks and made them the stars of such films as *The Great Locomotive Chase* and *The Brave Engineer*.

Whether budding entrepreneurs or crafty urchins, the news butchers had little to offer that could be considered good, nourishing food.

Cooking on Trains

Train crews faced the same food challenges as the passengers. However, they could take advantage of an oven of sorts. In the American West, train firemen fried buffalo steaks on their coal scoops. In Northern Ireland, as late as the 1950s, engine crews not only brewed their tea over the engine's coal fire, they cooked meals over it. Michael Hamilton, who worked on the Sligo, Leitrim & Northern Counties Railway, wrote:

> If a fry was on the menu a few hygiene regulations had to be observed. The fireman's coal shovel was washed clean with scalding water from the engine's boiler. When it was as clean as a hound's tooth, the rashers, eggs, sausages and black pudding were placed on it. Then, holding the shovel steady the cook gently thrust it into the hungry firebox with its flames ready to jump out at you. When the contents were done of one side, they were turned and in a matter of minutes the meal was ready for serving.[23]

Occasionally food was served, though not prepared, aboard trains in the years before 1867 when George M. Pullman introduced his hotel and dining cars. A crew might set up a counter and stools in a baggage car and sell simple food that had been prepared in a depot kitchen and kept warm in a steam box. Oyster stew, crullers, and coffee were typical offerings. During the Civil War, soldiers being transported on hospital trains were fed hot soup onboard.

In 1863, the Philadelphia, Wilmington & Baltimore Railroad introduced an early version of a restaurant car. Divided by a partition in its center, one-half of the car was used as a smoking section. In the other half, passengers ate at a counter. The food was prepared at a train terminal and was kept warm in a steam box.[24] The arrangement was more like a men's bar than a restaurant, and it is unlikely that any women ventured in for a meal.

Building the West

In settled areas, the railroad connected towns. In the American West, it created them. Wherever trains stopped, settlements sprang up. Initially, they were just a collection of hovels thrown together to house workers who were laying the rails. Along with worker housing, tents and wagons offering drink, gambling, and easy women flourished along the rails. The settlements were called "hell on wheels" because they were slapped together hastily as soon as the crews arrived and taken along to the next stop when they moved on.

Gradually more or less permanent settlements developed along the railway routes. Prospectors and prospective residents lived in flimsy shacks while they tried to find their fortunes. Most of the men who came from the East left their wives and families back home, hoping to have them travel to the West when and if it became more civilized. Only women of ill repute dared to live along the trail. At eating places waiters who were at best untrained and unkempt served bad food and fiery liquor in dirty surroundings to men who had forgotten any manners they ever had.

Clearly something needed to be done. As more people settled in the West, they needed better housing and decent places to eat. Frederick Henry Harvey had traveled enough to understand the problem. However, unlike other travelers, he saw the solution. Harvey had migrated from England to the United States in 1850, when he was fifteen. By the time he was twenty-two, he owned a café in St. Louis. Later, he worked in a restaurant, and then got a job as a mail clerk on the Hannibal & St. Joseph Railroad. He worked his way up to freight agent, a job that required him to travel throughout the Midwest during the workweek. His wife and children stayed home in Leavenworth, Kansas. His travels showed Harvey just how bad the food and lodging was, and he decided to do something about it.

Harvey convinced the owner of the Atchison, Topeka & Santa Fe Railroad that high-quality restaurants would be good for his railroad's business. The railroad followed the Santa Fe Trail, a commercial route that brought manufactured goods west and buffalo hides, fur, gold, and silver east. By 1872, it ran from Chicago to Colorado; it reached New Mexico six years later. It was the fastest growing railway in America, and its customers were hungry for decent meals. With a handshake, Charles F. Morse, superintendent of the railroad, and Harvey went into the railroad depot restaurant business in 1876. They agreed that Harvey would run the restaurants; the railroad would ship his provisions without charge; and if there was a profit, it would be Harvey's.

Harvey began by scrubbing the lunchroom space at the Topeka depot until it was spotless. When he opened the lunchroom, he made sure it served good, well-prepared food. He decreed that coffee would be made fresh every two hours. This was revolutionary in an area where the best anyone could hope for was coffee made once a day. He also insisted that his customers behave. Fred Harvey did not tolerate fighting, swearing, and spitting. Surprisingly, his customers agreed to his terms. Anything for a good meal.

The Harvey Girls sped up the civilizing process. Because male waiters were apt to drink and get into fights, Harvey hired young women from the East and the Midwest, "of good moral character," according to his newspaper ad for waitresses. He offered them $17.50 a month plus room and board and tips. It was less than a man would have made, but a decent salary for a woman in those days. Harvey Girls had to live in dormitories with supervision, wear modest uniforms, obey a curfew, and generally behave like ladies. In return, they received free train travel, a Western adventure, and independence from the limited opportunities for women in the East and Midwest. Even though waitressing was not seen as a respectable job for a woman, Harvey Girls came to be highly regarded. Eventually, despite the rules and curfews, many of them met and married ranchers or railroad men. It was said, not altogether in jest, that Harvey was running a matrimonial agency.[25]

Harvey's lunchroom in Topeka was just the beginning. In 1878, he took over the railway's hotel in the small Kansas town of Florence. He bought Irish linen tablecloths, English silver place settings, and fine china dishes. He hired a chef from the esteemed Palmer House in Chicago and paid him the bank-president sum of $5,000 a year. As he opened more restaurants and then hotels, the words "Harvey House" came to mean high quality in food, service, and surroundings.

The secret of the Harvey Houses' success was good food, prepared well and served properly. The food served at Harvey Houses was not the fine French cuisine of gourmet restaurants. Customers could pronounce the names of the foods on the menus, but were unaccustomed to such quality. Westerners who were used to tough, greasy fried buffalo steaks discovered

A group of Harvey Girls in Syracuse, Kansas, 1909. Courtesy of the Florence Historical Society and Harvey House Museum

tenderloin steaks shipped from Kansas City and served rare. Fruits and vegetables were always fresh. Harvey House cooks baked their own bread and squeezed fresh oranges for juice. They served local game and catch whenever it was available.

Typical Harvey menu items included shrimp cocktail, creamed onions, sugar-cured ham, beef stew, deviled lobster, roast Long Island duckling, and butterscotch pie Chantilly. Harvey Houses served regional specialties like old Virginia sour milk biscuits, huevos rancheros, cream of Wisconsin cheese soup, finnan haddie Dearborn, and New England pumpkin pudding. Harvey cooks followed the house recipes exactly so the dishes were consistent from place to place and time to time. Customers could also count on variety. Harvey menus were planned to make sure that railroad passengers who ate at several different Harvey Houses along a route never had to repeat a meal.

Harvey also understood the American need for speed. Thanks to efficient planning, a full meal and the famous Harvey coffee served by a polite, attractive Harvey Girl in a clean and relaxed environment could be enjoyed in a half an hour. Harvey arranged to have the conductors on the trains ask passengers if they planned to dine at the next station and if so, whether they preferred the dining room or the lunch counter. The conductors telegraphed the information ahead to the restaurant so that when the train stopped and the passengers entered, the tables would be set and the first course of either fresh fruit cups or salads would be ready. The restaurant manager would immediately carry a great platter of meat into the dining room and begin carving it into thick slices. Harvey Houses were known for their generous portions. Dessert pies were always sliced into four—rather than six—servings.

Then there was the seemingly magical Harvey beverage service. A Harvey Girl would ask the customers for their beverage orders, and then another server would come along and fill the orders correctly. All this was done without any communication between the servers. Customers were mystified, until the girls explained the code. The girl who took the order arranged the coffee cups according to a system that signaled the order to the one who served the beverages.

Cup upright in the saucer = coffee
Cup upside down in the saucer = hot tea
Cup upside down, tilted against the saucer = iced tea
Cup upside down, tilted away from the saucer = milk[26]

The system worked as long as the customer didn't move the cup.

Harvey was known as a tough taskmaster who would not tolerate anything that might damage the chain's reputation. Legend has it that when the manager of an unprofitable Harvey House found ways to cut losses from $1,000 a month to $500 by economies such as decreasing portion sizes, Harvey fired him. Whether true or not, the story—and people's belief in it—showed how serious Harvey was about maintaining his standards.

Over time, other good quality restaurants opened along American railroad routes in the West as well as the East. The Van Noy Railroad News Company, established in 1893, operated eating-houses and hotels along the Missouri Pacific Railway line. Like Harvey Houses, the Van Noy establishments were known for their high standards. But most rail station restaurants were not their equals. Hotel dining rooms were few and far between. Lunch baskets and snacks sold by news butchers were not sufficient. By the late nineteenth century, rail passengers wanted to eat well in clean, well-ordered surroundings on long trips, and they let the railway companies know it. The obvious solution was to provide them with good meals onboard trains.

The English Railway Sandwich

Stale and meager, the English railway sandwich was so vilified that it came to be a metaphor for poor quality and a rich source of jokes for comedians. But one of the most common offerings, egg and cress, is a delight when properly made and served fresh, rather than after it's been sitting in a rail station for several days.

✑ *Egg and Cress Sandwich*

2 slices of fresh bread
Mayonnaise
1 barely hard-boiled egg, chopped
Salt and pepper
Lots of fresh, crisp watercress

Spread each slice of bread with mayonnaise. Mix the chopped egg with a little mayonnaise and salt and pepper to taste. Top one slice of the bread with the egg mixture, then pile on a generous handful of cress. Top with the other slice of bread. Cut diagonally, in accordance with railway custom.

Pudding

Thomas Cook's "roast-beef-and-pudding-eating Englishman" was a subject of ridicule by some, but long before Cook's Tours were created, a seventeenth-century Frenchman, Henri Misson de Valbourg, wrote, "Ah, what a wonderful thing is an English pudding." The English do excel at pudding making. Their bread puddings vary from simple bread and butter puddings to elaborate ones that are fine enough for guests of the highest rank. They're called "diplomat" or "cabinet" puddings and are made with cake or ladyfingers, rather than plain bread, and layered with a rich custard and candied fruits.

This marmalade bread pudding is a simpler affair. It's perfect for breakfast or brunch because it may be made the night before you want to serve it, and simply popped into the oven and baked in the morning.

∾ Marmalade Bread Pudding

8–10 slices of bread with the crust removed. I like challah but any firm bread will do.
4 tablespoons softened butter
4 large eggs
2 cups whole milk
1 teaspoon vanilla
½ cup marmalade. Your favorite flavor. I like bitter orange.

Generously butter a one-quart baking pan. Cut bread into slices and butter them. Fit half of the bread slices into the pan butter side up, filling in any gaps with small pieces of bread. Spread with marmalade. Top with another layer of buttered bread.

Whisk the eggs, milk, and vanilla together. Pour over the bread. Cover with plastic wrap, pressing down to make sure all the bread is covered with the milk mixture. Refrigerate overnight or for several hours.

In the morning, preheat the oven to 350 degrees. Then remove the plastic wrap and put the pan into a larger pan. Pour hot water into the larger pan until it comes halfway to the rim of the pudding pan. Bake for 40–45 minutes or until the top is slightly puffed and browned. Remove bread pudding pan from the larger pan to serve.

CHAPTER 2

The Dining Car Debuts

When George M. Pullman named his first railroad dining car the *Delmonico* in 1868, he was sending a clear signal to potential passengers. This was to be fine dining. The New York restaurant of the same name was the most famous and esteemed in America. It was the restaurant that gave us Delmonico potatoes, lobster Newburg, chicken à la king, and baked Alaska. Princes of industry and royal princes alike dined at Delmonico's. Notables like Diamond Jim Brady and Lillian Russell began their dinners there by downing dozens of oysters, and then proceeded to enjoy a multicourse meal accompanied by fine wines.

Delmonico's was renowned for impeccable service, elegant décor, and most important of all, French cuisine. The menu, or *Carte du Restaurant Français*, was seven pages long, and was written in French as well as English, adding another note of sophistication to the scene. Selections included consommé or perhaps turtle soup to start. The fish course might be turbot or shad roe. It was followed by game and meats such as roast canvasback duck, pheasant, and mutton chops. Side dishes might include braised celery, tomato salad, beetroot salad, and mushroom patties. The dessert menu featured charlotte russe, soufflés, puddings, tarts, fresh fruit compotes, molded jellies, and ices. It was all accompanied by the appropriate wines. The menu listed more than fifty wines, as well as brandy, port, or Madeira, the fortified Portuguese wine that was so popular on nineteenth-century tables in the United States and in England.

This was hardly the sort of food or service the traveling public was accustomed to experiencing on a train; but Pullman promised and, ultimately, delivered it.

Pullman's Progress

Pullman already had a reputation for hard work and success when his *Delmonico* debuted in 1868. Although he left school after the fourth grade, he learned carpentry, furniture building, and house moving at his father's side in the small town of Brocton near Buffalo, New York, where he was born. Moving houses was a particularly good business there, since the expansion of the Erie Canal necessitated moving buildings back from its shore. In the 1850s, Pullman moved to Chicago and pioneered building-raising techniques there. The city was installing new sewer systems and roadways and required buildings, even multistory brick buildings, to be lifted up several feet to allow for the work to be done under them. Pullman was able to lift a building and then, after the systems were installed below, to lower it without rattling a window.

Despite his success, Pullman, still in his twenties, realized that real business growth was going to be in the emerging railroads. He had traveled enough to know that the existing sleeping cars left a lot to be desired. Their ceilings were so low that a man's head grazed them. The carriages were without ventilation, which was unpleasant at any time of year but particularly so in winter when a fire was going in the stove, and the car was filled with men who were overheated and unwashed. The beds were uncomfortable cots. Pullman believed he could do better. He and a business partner, Benjamin C. Field, a former New York state senator, began in 1859 by remodeling railroad cars to transform them into more comfortable sleepers. Several years later, Pullman designed a brand-new sleeping car and had it built. It was bigger, more comfortable, and more luxurious than any that had gone before. Named the *Pioneer*, it made its debut in 1865 on the Chicago, Alton & St. Louis Railroad.

With its rich black walnut interior, glittering chandeliers, plush upholstery, and elegant carpets, it set the standard for those that followed. The sleeping berths were comfortable, and one of their most impressive features was that they were made up with clean sheets. The lavatories featured marble washstands. Even in these beautiful surroundings, the tobacco chewers were still a problem. Many photographs and illustrations of elegant late nineteenth-century cars show spittoons placed on the floor next to each seat

Fine dining onboard an 1870 Pullman Hotel car. Courtesy of the Library of Congress

to protect the precious carpets in the hope that tobacco chewers could aim accurately.

Pullman was a master at generating positive publicity for his business. Before he introduced onboard food preparation and dining service, Pullman organized excursions for VIP passengers and press, and served them food that had been prepared at a railroad hotel and brought onboard. This is the menu, which was printed on silk, for an excursion on the Michigan Central; Chicago, Burlington & Quincy; and Chicago & North-Western railways on Saturday, May 19, 1866.

Geo. M. Pullman's Compliments.

Chicken Salad, Sandwiches
Strawberries and Cream
Assorted Cakes
Vanille, Lemon, and Strawberry Ice Cream
Lemon Ice, Orange Ice
Hockheimer. Rudesheimer. Braumberger
Chateau Margaux, Chateau Lafitte, and St. Julien
G.H. Mumm & Co.'s Dry Verzenay, Heidsieck
Moet & Chandon Green Seal, Widow Cliquot
Champagne Frappe
Sherry Cobblers, Claret Punch, Catawba Cobblers, Lemonade[1]

Pullman seldom drank himself, but he knew his guests did. He always made sure champagne and popular drinks of the day like sherry cobblers flowed liberally. Perhaps as a result, the news coverage of these expeditions was invariably good.

Pullman's business interests prospered and in 1867, his company was chartered as the Pullman Palace Car Company. His timing was perfect. The Gilded Age—with its ostentatious consumption, its love of display, its disdain for modesty and discretion in style—had begun. At the time, the average household income was decidedly un-golden at less than $400 a year; however, Pullman's customers were not average Americans. They were wealthy international travelers and businessmen who were making fortunes in postwar industrialization. They were ready to show the world just how successful they had become by traveling in palatial style.

In the same year, Pullman introduced another innovation—the hotel car—and put it into service on the Great Western Railroad of Canada. As the name implies, the hotel car offered all the amenities of a fine hotel aboard a train. Later, Henry James likened Pullmans to "rushing hotels" and compared hotels to "stationary Pullmans."[2] The hotel cars were as elegant as the sleepers, but with the added attraction of food service. The first one, which Pullman named the *President,* was sixty by ten feet in size and included a three by six foot kitchen with a coal stove. There was also a pantry, an icebox, and a wine closet. There was a cook and a porter doubled as a waiter.

During the day, passengers were seated in the car as usual. At mealtimes tables were fixed between the seats and set with fine china, glassware, silver, and linens invariably described as snowy. After the meals, the tables were removed. At night, the seats folded into lower sleeping berths and upper berths folded down from above them. The *Detroit Commercial Advertiser* of June 1, 1867, noted,

> The crowning glory of Mr. Pullman's invention is evinced in his success in supplying the car with a cuisine department containing a range where every variety of meats, vegetables and pastry may be cooked on the car, according to the best style of culinary art.[3]

Most passengers were excited by the idea of eating while traveling at the speed of thirty miles an hour, and they were impressed with the quality of the food. The first menu items included cold dishes—beef tongue, chicken salad, lobster salad, and sugar-cured ham. The cold dishes were a convenience since the kitchen was so small, but this was still the era before refrigeration so they did have to be kept on ice. Hot dishes included beefsteak, mutton chops, and ham, all served with potatoes. There was also Welsh rarebit; boiled, fried, or scrambled eggs; and plain or rum omelets. Although the dishes were more like home cooking than dishes served at fine dining restaurants of the era, passengers reported that the quality was excellent and the choices many.

William Fraser Rae, a *London Daily News* correspondent, described the hotel car in glowing terms in his account of an 1869 rail journey across the United States from New York to San Francisco.

> The first trip in one of these cars forms an epoch in a traveler's life. No royal personage can be more comfortably housed than the occupant of a Pullman car, provided the car be a hotel one. . . . At stated intervals the conductor walks around taking passengers' orders, who make their selections from the bill-of-fare.
>
> The choice is by no means small. Five different kinds of bread, four sorts of cold meat, six hot dishes, to say nothing of eggs cooked in seven different ways, and all the seasonable vegetables and fruits, form a variety from which the most dainty eater might easily find something to tickle his palate, and the ravenous to satisfy his appetite.[4]

Only the passengers in the hotel car ate there. Those in the other cars on the train had to either bring their own food aboard or hope to buy something at station stops. Rae, displaying a bit of *schadenfreude*, wrote: "An additional zest is given to the good things by the thought that the passengers in the other cars must rush out when the refreshment station is reached, and hastily swallow an ill-cooked meal."[5]

Clearly and despite protestations to the contrary, U.S. railway travelers were divided by class, just as passengers were in other countries. They were also divided by race. On some lines, black passengers were seated separately, sometimes in a section of the baggage car. Some Southern cities had separate waiting rooms at train stations as well.

Hotel car passengers paid $2.00 in addition to the regular fare, just as they did on the sleepers. They also had to pay an additional charge for the meals. Most passengers, possibly thinking of the quality of meals at the station stops, felt they were worth it. The English author of *Across the Ferry*, James Macaulay, traveling in a hotel car from Niagara Falls to Chicago in 1871 wrote:

> The bill of fare contained more variety than in many English hotels, and at moderate charges. For lamb chop or mutton chop and tomato sauce the price was seventy-five cents; fresh mackerel, fifty cents; omelet, with ham, forty; a spring chicken, a dollar. There was ample choice of vegetables, fruits, and relishes, with five or six kinds of wine, in the *carte*. A cup of French coffee, tea, or chocolate was fifteen cents.[6]

Most hotel car passengers described the cars as tasteful and elegant, and said the food was very good. But, as is always the case, some were not so pleased. The hotel car passengers sat, slept, and ate in the same carriage for the duration of their trip, which could be several days and nights. That caused some to complain about odors, boredom, and the manners and hygiene of the other passengers. As Macaulay put it, "You may be paired for a long period in too close proximity to an ineligible neighbor."[7]

Some passengers said that eating in a moving train made them experience motion sickness. In earlier years, passengers complained about soot on their clothes; now they were upset to find it drifting onto their food. Although many praised the food served, the menus were limited since the kitchen was small and cramped. Pullman had not realized his Delmonico dream yet.

The Dining Car

In 1868, just a year after the introduction of the first hotel car, Pullman introduced the dining car and called it the *Delmonico*. The dining car was a separate car with kitchen and dining facilities, exactly like a restaurant, but one that sped along a railroad track as diners enjoyed their meals. The *Delmonico* cost $20,000 to build, and operated on the Chicago & Alton Railroad running between Chicago and Springfield, Illinois.

In his patent application, Pullman called it a traveling dining-saloon and restaurant. The kitchen was located in the center of the car and was flanked by the dining areas. Pullman said he put the kitchen in the center so that

The dining car was a strong selling point for a railroad in the late nineteenth century. Courtesy of the Library of Congress

"in whatever direction the car may be travelling, at least one half of it will be in advance of the kitchen, the odors of which are borne by the draught toward the rear." He also thought having two dining areas made them more easily accessible from the other cars. When the dining car was located in the middle of the train, those seated in advance of the car could dine in the front section; those in one of the cars behind could dine in the rear section. Apparently, the middle of the car didn't prove to be as convenient a location since most subsequent dining cars had the kitchen at one end rather than in the middle.

Delmonico's kitchen measured eight by eight feet, still small, but larger than the kitchen on the hotel car. It included a water tank, a sink, a range, tables, and pantry storage space. Under the railroad car was a space Pullman called "a large refrigerator and provision-chamber." The refrigerator was actually a large icebox; the provision-chamber was where supplies of meats, fruits, vegetables, and other foods were stored. There was a door leading from it to the exterior of the car, so railroad employees could stock it at station stops without going through the car itself. A washroom and a water closet were located at each end of the car.

The car seated forty-eight in all at six tables for four in each dining area. A mirrored cabinet mounted on the wall between each set of seats contained what Pullman called "the table furniture"—that is, all the linens and silver for that table.[8]

Despite kitchen size constraints, railroad cooks managed to produce excellent meals, according to contemporary accounts. Courtesy of the Library of Congress

Staffing the Cars

With the advent of the dining car, it was no longer possible to simply have the conductor and porters do double duty; a dining car required a trained staff. On the *Delmonico*, two cooks and four waiters prepared and served up to 250 meals a day.[9] Later, depending on the train and the sophistication of the meals, a staff could consist of more than a dozen men: a steward who was responsible for supervising all dining services, an assistant steward, a chef, three or more cooks, and up to ten waiters. Pullman resolved the staffing issue by hiring recently freed house slaves. They were experienced and skilled at service, and he believed they would be polite and deferential to his passengers. Moreover, since they needed jobs, they would work for less money than whites. As discriminatory as his policy was, it did have some positive results. The Pullman Company became the largest employer of blacks in the country. Within the black community, working for Pullman meant steady employment, travel, and respect. One could take pride in wearing the Pullman uniform. Nevertheless, the men were underpaid and overworked even by the standards of the time.[10]

An article in the February 6, 1886 edition of *The New York Times* reported that it was "the general impression that Pullman car men are well paid by their employers for the work they do." But, the article continued, "this is very far from the actual state of the case." According to the article a porter on the New York to Chicago run could be on duty for thirty-seven hours without a rest. He earned just $19 a month, and out of that sum had to pay for his own meals, uniforms, and caps. Typically he had to buy two uniforms a year at a cost of $18 each. The expectation was that tips from passengers would make up for the low wages. Of course, not every passenger tipped generously, if at all. In addition, the workers were held responsible for the mistakes and mishaps of the passengers. If a passenger walked off with a Pullman comb or ashtray, whether mindlessly or with the intention of taking a souvenir home, the porter or waiter on duty would be charged for it. If the passenger broke a glass, the porter or waiter had to pay for it. The workers were powerless to complain.[11]

Some passengers treated the dining car crew with disdain. During the slavery era, it was common to call slaves by their owners' names rather than the name their parents had chosen for them. The practice carried over to the men who staffed the Pullman cars. Since Pullman's first name was George, many passengers called the porters and waiters "George," or they simply used another common name rather than take the trouble to learn what the person's name was. When Ellen Douglas Williamson was thirteen, in 1918,

In this 1901 illustration from the satirical magazine *Puck*, a thin Pullman porter shows the railroad president how low tips have sunk and asks for a regular salary. The plump porter in the inset represents the good old days of generous tips. Courtesy of the Library of Congress her family traveled on a Pullman train from Cedar Rapids to California. She kept a diary and in her innocence wrote:

> Another curious thing is that all Pullman porters were called George, unless you know them personally from former trips. They were also always black, as were the dining-car waiters, and a nicer, more courteous and pleasant group of men never existed.[12]

Years later, Lucius Beebe, an author and railroad aficionado who lived in the mid-twentieth century, described the practice in more adult terms:

> His name was George or Fred or Henry at the whim of the passenger and with only infrequent reference to the card in every car which proclaimed his proper given name, and he was an American institution. A man of infinite resources, limitless guile and the patience of Job, the Pullman porter had ridden a long way in the American legend.[13]

When a passenger did treat the men with respect, it was noted and appreciated. Jackie Gleason, the famed comedian of the 1950s and 1960s, was one of the men's favorites. He was known for his hundred-dollar tips and the party-like atmosphere on his private car, but more important they remembered him as one who treated them properly. He always called them by name and never referred to them as "George."[14]

Generally chief stewards and chefs were white and assistant cooks and waiters were black. But blacks did become chefs and were able to add dishes they knew and loved to the menu. In her book *The Welcome Table*, the historian Jessica B. Harris noted that Southern black dishes like pineapple fritters and cream of peanut soup made their way onto dining car menus in this way, much to the delight of passengers.

Some chefs became particular favorites of regular passengers and became well known in their own right. Pullman chef James Copper was Ignace Paderewski's favorite cook. The famed pianist arranged to have Copper cook on his private railroad car whenever he toured. When Copper retired, in 1928, *The New York Times* reported the event under the headline "Paderewski Chef quits Pullman Job. Overlord of Artist's Cuisine on tours for 25 years Retires Because of Age." It said that Copper considered his position one of great dignity "for if Paderewski was an artist in music, was not he, himself, an artist in foods?" The unnamed reporter not only used Copper's full name, he called him the "King of Cuisine."[15]

Delmonico Dining

The *Delmonico* and the dining cars that followed served meals that were said to be as good as those served at the finest hotels and restaurants and as plentiful. A dinner menu might include up to eighty dishes, from the ubiquitous oysters to wild game, fresh fish, roasts, and a variety of vegetables. There would be ices, cakes, and fruits to conclude. To drink, there were sherries, French wines, champagne, and Madeira as well as bottled mineral waters.

The tables were set with china designed for the line, usually featuring a company logo or a local theme. The Baltimore & Ohio's blue-and-white china depicted the Potomac Valley. The Great Northern Railroad's china featured its mascot, "Rocky" the Rocky Mountain goat, atop a crag with pine trees around the base. A pattern called Mimbreño, created in tribute to the Native American art of the Mimbres tribe, was used on the Atchison, Topeka & Santa Fe Railroad during the late 1930s. Dining car silver was often engraved with the name of the railroad and its coat of arms or logo. The glassware was fine crystal and it, too, might be engraved with a crest or particular design that identified it as belonging to the line.[16]

Adding to the air of indulgence, at dinnertime a smiling waiter would announce that the dining car was open by gently ringing C-F-A-C on the Deagan hand chimes, which looked rather like a small, handheld xylophone.

The service, the décor, and the food served on the dining cars all met with acclaim. A *New York Times* correspondent wrote an enthusiastic account of his trip from Omaha to San Francisco on the initial trip of two Pullman Palace cars (a dining car and a sleeper) across the continent in 1869. He said Pullman "has done more than all living men to lift railroad travel to the level of a fine art," and doubted that Delmonico himself could match the food. He wrote "O, muse of gastronomy, inspire me with language fitly to describe!"

Then he noted that dinner on the first night featured "in addition to all that ordinarily makes up a first-chop dinner," antelope steak, of which he said "the gourmet who has not experienced this—bah! What does he know of the feast of fat things?" There was also a delicious mountain brook trout, sauce "piquante and unpurchasable," and much more. It was all washed down with "bumpers of sparkling Krug." Later in the trip, he remarked, "we made twenty-seven miles in twenty-seven minutes, while our Champagne glasses filled to the brim spilled not a drop!"[17]

An article in the *New York Commercial Advertiser* on November 30, 1875 enthused: "The Pullmans . . . are able to make a bill of fare and serve it in a style which would cause Delmonico to wring his hands in anguish."[18]

If dinners were lavish, breakfasts were no less substantial. In his book, *A Scamper Through America,* published in 1882, an English writer, T.S. Hudson, included the menu for breakfast on a train going westward from Cincinnati.

BREAKFAST
Now Ready, Served in first-class Style, 75 cents
A DINING CAR is attached to this train. "Eat and be satisfied!"
PASSENGERS Will appreciate this new feature of "Life on the Road."
BREAKFAST BILL OF FARE.
English Breakfast Tea. French Coffee. Chocolate. Ice Milk.
BREAD
French Loaf. Boston Brown Bread. Corn Bread. Hot Rolls. Dry, Dipped,
    Cream and Buttered Toast.
BROILED
Tenderloin Steak, plain or with Mushrooms. Spring Chicken. Mutton
    Chops. Veal Cutlets. Sirloin Steak. Sugar-Cured Ham.
GAME IN THEIR SEASON
OYSTERS IN THEIR SEASON
FRIED
Calf's Liver with Bacon. Country Sausage. Trout.
EGGS
Fried. Scrambled. Boiled. Omelets. Plain.
RELISHES
Radishes. Chow Chow. French Mustard. Worcestershire Sauce. Currant
    Jelly. Mixed Pickles. Horse Radish. Tomato Catsup. Walnut Catsup.
VEGETABLES
Stewed, Fried, and Boiled Potatoes.
FRUITS
Apples. Oranges.

Hudson was not as hyperbolic a writer as the *Times* correspondent. He merely wrote, "We partook of a good breakfast, cooked and served on the train."[19]

Local Foods

Many railroad lines became famous for serving local products and signature dishes in their dining cars. Passengers traveling to the West for the first time might be introduced to buffalo, antelope steak, pheasant, sage hen, or mountain sheep. On the East Coast, they could count on New England clam chowder and Boston baked beans. Pennsylvania lines served fried Philadelphia scrapple, a spiced pork and cornmeal sausage, and shoofly pie, a typical Pennsylvania Dutch pie made with molasses. The Michigan Central featured Lake Michigan whitefish and also Michigan ice cream, presumably made with fresh local milk. The Southern Pacific served California sand dabs. The Baltimore & Ohio was known for its corn bread and country sausage breakfast.

Potatoes achieved prominence on the Northern Pacific Railroad. In 1909, the company's superintendent, Hazen Titus, learned that potato growers in Washington's Yakima Valley were using their giant potatoes as hog feed because customers wouldn't buy them. So he did some experimenting. He discovered that baking the two-pound potatoes for two hours resulted in the lightest, fluffiest baked potato he'd ever had. So he put them on the menu of the *North Coast Limited* as the "GREAT BIG BAKED POTATO," and charged ten cents a serving. They became an instant hit and one of the most famous of the railroad's specialties. Over the years, the line sold potato premiums ranging from postcards to aprons, and organized a "Great Big Baked Potato Booster Club" complete with membership certificates for dining car patrons. In 1914, Titus had a forty-foot long, eighteen-foot diameter potato built atop its commissary in Seattle. Lit up at night, the eyes of the potato winked and the butter pat on its top glowed.[20]

On some trains, even the bottled waters might be local. An undated breakfast menu from the Dixie Flyer offering service from the Midwest to Florida in the late nineteenth and early twentieth century included this information about the water served aboard the train, "We serve on this car the celebrated Highland Club Water, from the famous springs of the Highland Club, White Bluff, Tenn. This water contains only fifteen grains of solids per gallon, and is certified bacteriologically pure."[21]

Local or regional was not always the case. A menu from the Southwestern Railway, nicknamed the "Cotton Belt Route," listed Boston baked beans and English plum pudding among its offerings. The Santa Fe offered spring chicken, Maryland-style. Boston brown bread was served on the Michigan Central menu.

Other dishes were ubiquitous on both restaurant and dining car menus in the late nineteenth century. Oysters—raw, fried, stewed, roasted, in the omelet known as "Hangtown fry," and in fried oyster "po' boy" sandwiches— were eaten wherever and whenever they were in season. Oyster popularity was at its zenith in the nineteenth century. Oysters were served for breakfast, lunch, and dinner, in basement saloons, at street stands, at Boston's famed

Union Oyster House,[22] and at Delmonico's restaurant in New York. Transporting them from the coasts to inland cities was a problem, however, until Arthur E. Stilwell—the founder of the Kansas City Southern Railway—invented and patented the Stilwell Oyster Car in 1898. The car, manufactured by the Pullman Company, contained six separate insulated tanks. The oysters were loaded into the tanks through openings in the top of the car. Then seawater was poured into each one. When the train arrived at its destination, the oysters were unloaded from chutes on the side of the car. On August 16, 1898, the *Chicago Tribune* reported:

> Gourmands who live in the heart of America, far, far removed from the haunt of the succulent bivalve, can now have their oysters fresh as though they lived on the seashore. . . . This experiment has proven so successful that the railroads all over the country are going to adopt it, so that fresh oysters can be a feature of every table in the near future.[23]

That was the problem. Oysters were so popular that the oyster beds on both the East and West coasts were nearly depleted. Oysters became scarce and expensive. Twenty-first-century aquaculture methods are bringing oysters back, but they are not as plentiful or as affordable as they once were.

Green turtle soup was also common on nineteenth-century menus—in restaurants, hotels, and trains. As a result, the turtles became an endangered species. Because they were large and cumbersome to prepare, many recipes suggested using canned turtle meat rather than fresh. Escoffier himself suggested in his *Ma Cuisine* that it was easier to buy the soup ready-made.[24] Mock turtle soup was made with calves' heads in place of turtles. That's why John Tenniel's image of the Mock Turtle in *Alice in Wonderland* has a calf's head, hind hoofs, and tail. But when the Mock Turtle sang "Beautiful soup, so rich and green, Waiting in a hot tureen," it was the real, not the mock, he extolled.

Despite the reputation dining cars had for serving local and regional foods, ultimately the railroad was responsible for much of the homogenization of the national diet. By making it possible to ship foods across the country quickly, the railroads erased seasonality and local sourcing from America's tables. The railroad brought California's produce to the East Coast, Florida's oranges to everyone. Northern states no longer had to wait for summer to enjoy strawberries or tomatoes. They could have them anytime. It's true that the railroad made greater varieties of foods more available and more affordable. There was a decided benefit in convenience and accessibility, but the cost was a loss of flavor and the decline of the family farm. Over time, the railroad helped turn agriculture into agribusiness.

The Transcontinental Railroad

In 1869, just a year after the *Delmonico* made its debut, a golden spike was hammered into the rail at Promontory Summit, Utah joining the Union Pacific and Central Pacific rail lines and forming the country's first transcontinental railroad. Now freight, business travelers, and tourists could be transported all the way from cities on the East Coast to the West, from New York to California. Long-distance travel was faster and easier than ever before. Clearly, this meant that more trains offering sleeping and eating accommodations were going to be needed. One would expect that railroads would be eager to add dining cars. The market was ready. The dining cars had received enthusiastic praise in the press and from those who had dined in them. In August 1868, *Harper's Weekly* magazine declared:

> The demand for rapid travelling . . . has led to the abandonment of many stops at lunch rooms and stations. The cry: "Wilmington, fifteen minutes for refreshments!" is no longer heard, but instead the passenger enjoys his soup, his fish, his joint, Clicquot [champagne] and coffee while the train runs fifty miles an hour."[25]

Dining cars were a strong selling point for the lines that did carry them. As early as 1869, the Chicago, Rock Island & Pacific Railroad ran an ad pointing out that it was "The Only Line of Dining and Restaurant Cars . . . between Chicago and Omaha."[26] Other lines ran ads touting their sleeping, dining, and/or buffet service, often specifically emphasizing that it was provided by Pullman, whose name already stood for quality.

Given all the positive response from passengers and press, were railroad owners inclined to add dining cars? They were not. In fact some made agreements that they would not add dining cars if their competitors would also refrain. In 1881, the Chicago, Burlington & Quincy Railroad Company; the Atchison, Topeka & Santa Fe Railroad Company; and the Union Pacific Railway Company signed an agreement saying none of them would run dining or hotel cars on their routes without giving the others six months advance notice. But a newcomer, the Northern Pacific Railroad Company, was not part of the agreement. When that company completed its line between Duluth and Portland in 1883, it ran with dining cars. The Chicago, Burlington & Quincy withdrew from the agreement a year later. By 1891, the need to compete successfully for passengers forced all western transcontinental lines to add dining cars.[27]

Railroad companies had resisted because the dining car was an expensive car to build and to run. A simple passenger car, however ornately decorated, was essentially a box with seating. But a dining car required specialized equipment and furnishings. There was the kitchen itself, with its stove, grill, iceboxes, pantry space, cooking and service equipment and, of course, food and drink. In the dining area, there was the cost of specially designed china, glassware, silver, and linens, as well as dining tables and chairs. Passengers expected the dining area to be beautifully designed, which meant incurring the expense of hiring fine woodworkers and artists to create the décor. In addition, the car was not occupied by paying customers except during meal times. The car itself could weigh up to eighty tons and, in the late nineteenth century, could cost $15,000 or more, three times the cost of a typical coach car. The elegant *Delmonico* cost $20,000. The china, linens, and other equipment could cost up to another $12,000.[28] Staffing was also expensive despite the low wages.[29]

The price of a dinner was usually seventy-five cents to a dollar, about the same as most hotel or restaurant meals at the time. Even when diners ordered à la carte and the total paid increased, it did not cover the cost to the railroad. As much as they tried to avoid it, the railroads had to capitulate to customers' desires, particularly because it was the first-class customer who insisted on dining onboard rather than at the station refreshment rooms. In addition, trains were faster by the 1880s, and it was increasingly difficult to coordinate station stops with optimum times for dining. Rather than build new station dining areas, most railroads opted to acquire dining cars. Even the Santa Fe, a holdout both because of its agreement with the other two railroads and its connection to Harvey Houses, finally began to run dining cars catered by Fred Harvey. The Harvey name was always prominent on the menus. This luncheon menu dated November 9, 1899 included the message, in capital letters: "YOU ARE PARTICULARLY REQUESTED TO REPORT ANY INATTENTION TO FRED. HARVEY, UNION DEPOT, KANSAS CITY MO."[30]

LUNCHEON
Potage, St. Germain
Watercress
Radishes
Sweetbreads, Glace, a la Villeroi
Spring Chicken, Maryland-Style
Cold Meats
Roast Beef
Ham
Imported Sardines

Welsh Rarebit
Potatoes—Persilade, or Baked Sweet
Endive Salad
Cream of Caramel
Chocolate Eclairs
Brie Cheese
Toasted Crackers
Coffee

The era of the elaborate dining car had begun and despite their initial reluctance, the railroads built increasingly elegant and even ostentatious cars and served lavish meals. The losses incurred came to be seen as the price of doing business. Railroad owners thought that passengers, particularly businessmen, who were impressed by the excellence of the food and service would subsequently trust that line with their freight and other business. In other words, they thought the losses would be made up by their public relations value.

The losses were substantial. In *The American Railroad Passenger Car*, John H. White Jr., curator and senior historian of the Division of Transportation, Smithsonian Institution, wrote that in 1887 each dining car lost approximately $100–600 a month; some railroads lost as much as $20,000 a year.[31]

Innovations

In 1883, Pullman introduced buffet cars to give passengers a place to have light snacks between meals when the dining car was closed. The early buffet cars were located between the smoking car and the drawing room and offered tea and coffee, oyster stew, boiled eggs, cold chicken, and other light refreshments. Some parlor cars included a built-in buffet area offering the same kinds of food. The buffets' purpose was to complement dining cars, not replace them. But some passengers preferred the lighter, more casual meals in the buffets to the formal multicourse menus of the dining cars. Over time, buffet cars would come to outnumber dining cars. For the railroad companies, the buffet had the advantage of being less expensive to staff and maintain than dining cars.

In 1887, another improvement in rail service and, indirectly, dining took place. Walking from a seat in a coach car to one in a dining car on a moving train was a risky proposition, especially in bad weather. For years, railroads had been trying to make the connections between individual cars safer and

easier for their passengers and had experimented with various inventions. None had been completely successful. Finally, Henry Howard Sessions, the superintendent of Pullman's Chicago plant, designed and patented an enclosed vestibule. Passengers could walk from the car they were seated in to the dining car without fear. No longer were they confined to one area during a long trip. They could stroll to the library car to read or to the lounge to chat with fellow passengers, or visit the barber for a shave, all without risking life and limb. The Pullman Company ran ads emphasizing the safety of the vestibule train. According to one, it "not only afforded comfort and safety to passengers" but cleanliness was also one of its virtues. "No longer was the opening of the forward door accompanied by a blast of wind heavy with smoke and cinders."[32] Vestibule trains soon became a hallmark of first-class travel. As the writer Moses King put it:

> When one grows weary of looking at the changing landscape through broad windows of transparent plate glass he may walk forward securely through the cars and their vestibuled connections to the library car with its fine shelves of books and periodicals and its desks all supplied with stationery for people who want to write letters or telegrams. The train also has its comfortable lounging places for smokers who may purchase their nicotinous sedatives there and an artist in liquids stands ready to fabricate every variety of the cup which cheers.[33]

This is the menu from a "Pullman Vestibuled Train," dated June 5, 1897.[34]

DINNER
Puree of Split Pea
Consomme, Clear
Cucumbers
Olives
Baked Pickerel, A La Creole
Pommes, Parisienne
Game Pie
Banana Fritters, Vanilla Flavor
Prime Roast Beef
Spring Lamb, Mint Sauce
Boiled Potatoes
Mashed Potatoes
New Peas
Fresh Shrimp Salad, Au Mayonnaise
Blanc Mange, A La Vanille

Apple Pie
Assorted Cake
Ice Cream
Fruit
Roquefort Cheese
Edam Cheese
Café Noir

Of course, Pullman was not the only innovator in the railroad business. Others built stylish sleepers and dining cars, buffets, and parlor cars. They all catered to the same well-to-do passenger. But Pullman was the best known both in the United States and abroad, and eventually the Pullman Company controlled most of the U.S. luxury train market.

So it was only natural that when a wealthy Belgian train enthusiast arrived in the United States in 1867, he traveled on Pullman trains. He enjoyed their fine dining, comfortable sleeping arrangements, and luxurious surroundings. He was so impressed with the Pullman quality and style that he determined to create similar cars in Europe. His name was Georges Nagelmackers and, inspired by Pullman, he went on to create the Compagnie Internationale des Wagons-Lits, and its famous *Orient Express*.

Pickles

Pickling—preserving vegetables or fruits in a vinegar or brine solution—has been relied on to provide nutritious food during lean times since antiquity. Valued for their keeping quality, pickles are enjoyed for their flavor, which may be sour, sweet, salty, or spicy. Especially during the nineteenth century, pickles were popular in delicatessens, restaurants, hotels, on trains, and at home. A cupboard full of jars of pickled vegetables was common in households before refrigeration, when home cooks routinely canned, pickled, and preserved.

During the latter half of the nineteenth century, the mixed vegetable pickle known as chow chow was particularly popular. It appeared on nearly every menu from hotels and restaurants to steamships and railways. Prized for its appetizing tanginess and its keeping qualities, it was featured in cookbooks intended for home use during the same era as well. However, by 1940, it had all but disappeared from both menus and cookbooks.

Home cooks' recipes were typically for large quantities of vegetables including cucumbers, cauliflower, cabbage, onions, green peppers, and green tomatoes. One called for two hundred small cucumbers; another, for a large cabbage and two gallons of cucumbers cut in pieces the size of the end of one's little finger. Cutting up all those vegetables into tiny pieces was time-consuming as was the rest of the preparation. Most often the vegetables were salted, then soaked overnight, then boiled the next day, and finally, canned.

The following simpler chow chow comes from *Jenny June's American Cookery Book*, published in 1870 and written by Jane Cunningham Croly. Born in England in 1829, Croly moved with her family to the United States when she was twelve and began working as a journalist in New York when she was twenty-five. In just three years, she had her own syndicated column, probably the first women in the United States to do so. Her writings encompassed cooking, women's rights, and education, and she was one of the founders of the General Federation of Women's Clubs.

∽ Handy Chow Chow

Chop together very finely a head of cabbage, 6 green peppers, 6 green tomatoes, add 2 tea-spoonsful of mustard, sufficient salt, vinegar to wet it, and if desired a little cloves and allspice. It is ready then for use and will keep a long time. No better appetizer can be made.

Another popular pickle of the period was made from watermelon rind. Since watermelon was so widely consumed in summer, pickling its rind was a thrifty way to use the entire fruit. It still is. This is a contemporary recipe from Patricia Kelly, author of *Luncheonette: Ice-Cream, Beverage, and Sandwich Recipes from the Golden Age of the Soda Fountain* (1989), used with her permission.

∽ Watermelon Rind Pickle

2 cups watermelon rind, red flesh and outer skin removed, cut into ½-to-1-inch pieces
1 tablespoon salt
1 cup cider vinegar
1 cup sugar
1 cinnamon stick, cracked
¼ tablespoon whole cloves
¼ tablespoon whole allspice
½-inch piece of ginger, sliced

Combine the prepared rind with two cups of water and one tablespoon of salt. Let soak overnight.

Drain rind, but do not rinse.

Combine vinegar and sugar in a pot. Tie spices up in a square of cheesecloth and add to the vinegar mixture. Bring to a boil, stirring to dissolve the sugar. Lower the heat. Add the watermelon rind and simmer for one hour.

Remove spice bag, but do not drain the liquid. Pour into a container and store in the refrigerator.

This is particularly good as an accompaniment to Manchego or aged Pecorino cheeses.

CHAPTER 3

Fine Dining on
European Railroads

The *Orient Express*. The name conjures up images of women fashionable in furs and jewels, men in black tie, and multilingual conversations over martinis. At dinner, the champagne sparkles and flows. Caviar glistens in the lamplight. There may be a famous author on the train or a murderer or, at the very least, a member of a royal family traveling incognito with someone other than a spouse. Is the couple at the next table in the dining car whispering sweet nothings or state secrets?

No train captured the imagination in quite the same way as the *Orient Express*, nor inspired so many novels and films. No wonder the myths and the facts are so interwoven as to be nearly impossible to separate completely. Even the name isn't entirely accurate. The company Georges Nagelmackers created in 1872 was called the Compagnie Internationale des Wagons-Lits (International Sleeping-Car Company), not the *Orient Express*. The train that ran between Paris and the city then called Constantinople (now Istanbul) was called the *Express d'Orient*, which was translated to *Orient Express*. The name became official in 1911 and came to be commonly used for different routes and different trains, and even as a generic term for European luxury travel.

During the late nineteenth and early twentieth centuries, tourism and travel were becoming more prevalent among the European elites just as they were among Americans. The word *hospitality* no longer simply meant a welcoming manner; it named an industry. César Ritz and Auguste Escoffier, hotelier and chef respectively, led the way. Together they transformed hotels and restaurants and created an international style that catered to the wealthy traveler. They worked together in all the right places—Monte Carlo, London, Rome, Paris—and wherever they went, the fashionable followed.

Ritz brought such innovations to European hotels as private baths, telephones, electric lights, fine linens, and high-quality furnishings. He understood that the new, wealthy class of travelers wanted to have their every wish anticipated and granted. He also realized that grand hotels required nothing less than grand restaurants. Escoffier had trained in the French apprenticeship system, and when Ritz offered him a job at the Grand Hôtel in Monte Carlo in 1884, he was ready. Still in his thirties, he had already worked in restaurants and hotels in the south of France and in Paris. During the Franco-Prussian War, he cooked for the army in several locations. After the war, when he was just twenty-seven, he became the head chef at the Petit Moulin Rouge in Paris. While there, and subsequently at other restaurants in Paris and on the Riviera, he developed a reputation for excellence and a loyal following.

Although his training was in classic cuisine, Escoffier brought his own ideas and imagination to his dishes and began moving away from the overly opulent dining of forebears like the famed Antonin Carême. Escoffier's menus seem lavish today, but they were much more restrained than those of earlier French chefs. He eliminated the elaborate garnishes of the past, and stressed flavor over flamboyance while still creating stylish presentations. He also knew how to curry favor with the famous by inventing and naming special dishes for them. One of his best-known creations was Pêche Melba, created for the famous opera star Nellie Melba when she was starring in the opera *Lohengrin*. Pêche Melba is a good example of the way he created flavorful dishes and presented them with enough flair to impress even the most jaded guest. Originally Pêche Melba was poached fresh peaches set on rich vanilla ice cream, topped with a swirl of spun sugar and served in a graceful swan carved from ice. Later the dish came to be topped with fresh raspberry sauce and the ice swan disappeared. Naming dishes after famous patrons was one way Escoffier, and other chefs, built up a clientele.

Escoffier reorganized the professional kitchen, making it much more functional. Each cook had his own specialty, from making sauces to preparing cold dishes, from sautéing to making pastry. The system eliminated duplication of effort and brought new efficiency to the kitchen. It also allowed cooks working in small kitchens—like those on trains—to work more productively. His system became the norm in restaurants all over the world. Escoffier's dishes gained fame throughout Europe, thanks in part to his own travels and writings and in part to his many wealthy and well-traveled clients. His influence also grew because of the many cooks he trained, who then trained others who worked in restaurants, hotels, ocean liners, and railways. Escoffier's version of haute cuisine influenced menus all over the world.

Setting New Standards

The expectations created by Ritz and Escoffier in Europe and by Delmonico and Pullman in the United States were the standards Nagelmackers aspired to with his new company. He was accustomed to fine dining at restaurants and hotels in Europe, but for the most part, European trains were not as luxurious. During his travels in the United States in 1867–1868, Nagelmackers had been so impressed by the elegance of Pullman sleeping cars and dining cars that he determined to bring the same level of refinement to European railways.

This was no simple task. Each European country had its own language, its own standards, and its own Machiavellian political intrigues. The leaders of some countries considered trains to be military assets and did not want their neighbors and potential enemies to be able to use captured rail stock. They were more interested in preventing trains from crossing borders than making it easy for them to do so. Trains could not simply run across Europe the way they could run across America. Passengers traveling through one European country to another typically had to get off the train before the border, go through border security, walk over to another train, and then resume the trip. Nagelmackers wanted his passengers to be able to travel across borders as seamlessly as if they were relaxing in their own home or in a fine hotel. That meant that he had to convince the leaders of the various countries' railways to cooperate. The best way to do that, he knew, was to enlist royal patronage.

Nagelmackers solicited the support of a family friend, Belgian king Leopold II. The king was a train enthusiast and, equally important, he was related to nearly every crowned head in Europe. Queen Victoria was his cousin; his father-in-law was the Archduke Joseph of Austria; and on the other side of the Atlantic, his sister Carlota was empress of Mexico. The king, who was later to become infamous for his cruelty and exploitation of the people of the Congo, lent his name and royal prestige to the business, but not his money. In fact, years later Nagelmackers had to build, at his own expense, a private rail car lavish enough to suit the taste of Leopold's favorite mistress, Caroline Lacroix. Nevertheless, the star power of a royal patron was worth its cost. The Wagons-Lits Company always appealed to the rich and glamorous, the famous, and the infamous.

Nagelmackers was inspired by Pullman, but he adapted his operation to European sensibilities. He knew that the open planning of American trains would not suit well-to-do European travelers. They wanted privacy, closed compartments, and separate accommodations for their servants. They also wanted elegant dining of the sort they were accustomed to enjoying in London or Paris.

The Trial Run

After many problems and delays, not the least of which was the Franco-Prussian War, Nagelmackers scheduled a trial run with a dining car from Paris to Vienna in October 1882. He and invited guests left the Gare de Strasbourg in Paris on Tuesday, October 10, and arrived in Vienna a day later, having traveled the nearly 839 miles in twenty-eight hours. The train was called the *Train Éclair de Luxe*, or lightning luxury train, despite its less than thirty mile an hour speed. It bore the company's impressive bronze logo featuring two lions and the company's newly expanded name, Compagnie Internationale des Wagons-Lits et des Grands Express Européens.

The train's most notable feature was its restaurant car. The meals were much like those one would expect at the time in a fine restaurant or hotel, but since they were prepared and served onboard a moving train, they were much more impressive.

For dinner, there were the ever-present oysters and then soup, followed by a fish course. The fish served on this occasion, turbot, was so popular at the time that it was nicknamed *le roi du carême* (the king of lent).[1] The menu doesn't indicate how it was cooked, but turbot was generally poached. It is so large that it has its own specially designed poacher, called a *turbotière*. A diamond-shaped, covered pan usually made of copper, it is designed to accommodate the fish's unusual diamond shape and large size. A turbot can be forty inches long and weigh up to fifty pounds. The turbot was served with a green sauce, likely to have been a mayonnaise made with fresh green herbs such as chervil, parsley, watercress, and spinach.

Other dishes included chicken à la chasseur—braised chicken with mushrooms, shallots, tomatoes, and white wine. There was a filet of beef with château potatoes, potatoes sautéed in butter. A *chaud-froid* of game was also served. The term *chaud-froid*, or hot-cold, refers to a dish that is prepared as a hot dish, sauced, and then glazed with aspic and served cold. A popular menu item at the time, it is a decorative presentation that has the advantage of advance preparation. The meal concluded with a dessert buffet.

A year later, in 1883, the *Express d'Orient* made its debut run from Paris to Constantinople. Nagelmackers was thirty-eight years old, and this was the trip he'd been preparing for ever since his visit to the United States.

An exuberant crowd gathered at the Gare de l'Est in Paris to see the train off. After the requisite champagne toasts and extended speeches, the train finally pulled out of the station. Its passengers reflected the international nature of the route. Nagelmackers welcomed government officials from France, Belgium, and the Ottoman Empire along with bankers, railway executives, and writers. Like Pullman, Nagelmackers understood the importance of good press. He made sure writers were onboard to help publicize the trip and provided plenty of champagne to inspire them. On this trip, they included two of the most popular writers of the day, Edmond About, a best-selling French author, and Henri Opper de Blowitz, the Paris correspondent of the *London Times*.

The train was made up of a locomotive, a mail car, three sleeping cars, a restaurant car, and a baggage car. Because the kitchen wasn't large enough to hold all the supplies needed for the extravagant dining planned for the trip, the baggage car did double-duty. In addition to containing the passengers' luggage, it was equipped with an icebox that held supplies of food, wine, champagne, and liqueurs.[2]

The cars' exteriors were royal blue with gilt lettering. The sleeping cars' interiors had walls of teak and mahogany paneling with inlaid designs on the car doors and compartment walls. The damask drapes at the windows could be tied back with silk cords with golden tassels so that passengers could enjoy the passing scenery. The seats were upholstered in soft leather and, at night, were converted to beds.[3] Each compartment had a bell to call the attendant when needed and a speaking tube to communicate with the conductor who was always seated at the end of the car.

The restrooms, located at the end of each car, featured marble fixtures and porcelain washbowls. Fresh towels, soaps, and toilet water were all at hand. An attendant was stationed outside the restroom door, ready to tidy the room after a passenger used it so that it was always spotless for the next visitor.

The restaurant car included a drawing room for ladies with tapestry-covered walls, an embroidered chaise lounge, elegant chairs and side tables, and lovely silk draperies. Although there were no women aboard the first leg of the trip, two joined the train in Vienna. At the other end of the car was a club-like smoking room for the men. It was furnished with leather armchairs and bookcases filled with books, maps, travel guides, and newspapers from the various countries on the route.

Dining aboard one of the famed *Orient Express* cars in 1883. Courtesy of the Bridgeman Art Library

Photographs show a dining area in the ornate style of the era with walls of paneled and carved mahogany, teak, and rosewood, and a clerestory decorated with paintings. Watercolors and etchings were mounted between the windows. The room was lit with the soft flattering glow of gas chandeliers. On one side, there were tables for four; on the other, tables for two, seating a total of forty-two. The flowers on the tables were fresh, the Baccarat crystal glasses sparkled, the tableware was solid silver, and the porcelain plates were embellished with the company's golden emblem.

The menu for dinner on the inaugural run listed ten courses from soups to sorbets, from caviar to capon, fruits, fine wines, and naturally, champagne. The food was prepared by a chef from Burgundy not named in the reports but reputed to be a large man with a black beard.[4]

Wagons-Lits Staffing

Like concierges at fine hotels, Wagons-Lits staff handled everything from bookings to unraveling the intricacies of international routes, from making sure a passenger and his luggage arrived at their destination together to recommending the best fishing spot in Sarajevo. Customs inspections were managed onboard the train, usually without disturbing passengers or their luggage. Previously, as one traveler put it, inspections made "a salad of the contents of one's bags."[5]

Every employee, regardless of position, was expected to be skilled, polite, and resourceful. No matter how demanding passengers were, the employees were to treat them with deference and courtesy and to meet all their demands. From the beginning, the Wagons-Lits staff was impressive. It was headed by a *chef de brigarde* or *chef de train*, not a cook but a manager of the sleeping and dining cars, a position rather like the general manager of a fine hotel today. The *chef de train* knew who his passengers were and what their needs might be. He knew basic first aid and was able to smooth out any problems that arose.

Next in importance was the *maître d'hotel* who supervised the dining car staff. In photographs, servers are outfitted in morning coats, knee breeches with white stockings, and buckled shoes. They look like palace footmen. After the turn of the century, the men wore official royal blue railroad uniforms trimmed in gold and looked more like military officers.[6]

More than their appearance, the language skills of the staff impressed travelers. They were expected to speak at least three languages, usually French, German, and English, and many spoke more than three. In 1894, the staff sent a telegram offering New Year's greetings to Nagelmackers, with each member telegraphing in his own language. The company's London manager, Mr. H. M. Snow, reported that the greeting was transmitted in fifty languages and dialects.[7]

The *chef de cuisine* headed the kitchen staff of sous-chefs, cooks, and cleaners. Wagons-Lits chefs were very often French and were considered the equal of chefs at the best hotels and restaurants of the day. The chefs were supposed to be able to provide even the most finicky and demanding passengers with anything they desired. It was even said that the chefs could provide kosher or halal meals for passengers who required them. Passengers often tried to tempt the chefs into leaving the railroad to work in private homes or exclusive restaurants. According to popular lore, they inevitably refused.

All Wagons-Lits staff members were expected to be discreet. If Monsieur X was seen traveling with Madame Y, rather than his wife, no word of this was to be mentioned by the sleeping car attendant. Secrets, state or personal, might be overheard but they were not to be repeated. Discretion was prized and passengers rewarded it handsomely. As a result, some railway staff were able to open their own restaurants or inns when they left the company. Others enjoyed a comfortable retirement.[8]

First-Class Travel

The first Paris-to-Constantinople trains were exclusively first class and travel on them was very expensive. The round-trip fare in the 1880s was sixty pounds.[9] That was more than the average yearly salary of the passengers' servants.[10]

The first trip was not quite the smooth and seamless success that it was reputed to be or that later trips would become. After the passengers boarded the train in Paris, they proceeded to Munich, then Vienna, and then Giurgiu in Romania. The trip took a long time because of all the receptions and celebrations at stops along the way. When they arrived at Giurgiu, the passengers had to leave the train and transfer to a ferry to cross the Danube to Ruse, Bulgaria. There, they boarded an ordinary—not a luxury Wagons-Lits—train and traveled to Varna on the coast. Then they boarded a steamship that took them along the Black Sea to finally reach Constantinople. According to a *Time Magazine* article published in 1960, the trip of "2,000-odd miles took six days and six hours, what with all the border ceremonies and crowds along the track."[11]

Still, the 1883 trip was so well received that business prospered and Nagelmackers proceeded to add new trains and new routes. By 1889, the train went directly to Constantinople without the need for switching trains or transferring to ships. To make sure *Orient Express* passengers would continue to be cosseted when they reached their destination; in 1892 the company constructed the Pera Palace Hotel in Constantinople. Two years later, Nagelmackers founded the Compagnie Internationale des Grand Hotels and began operating deluxe hotels in cities including Cairo, Nice, Lisbon, and Ostend. By the end of the century, the company's trains linked all the important capitals of Europe, with the exception of London. Its 550 cars traveled more than 90,000 miles a day and carried nearly 2,000,000 passengers a year to and from Lisbon, Madrid, Paris, Rome, Vienna, and St. Petersburg.

A new *train de luxe*, the *Rome Express*, running from Calais to Rome, made its debut in 1897. An English businessman, who was not identified by name, writing in *Railway Magazine* that December, described his first trip on the new train in glowing terms. In fact, he was so impressed with it that he concluded his description by writing "Merci, Monsieur Nagel-mackers!" He noted approvingly that the train was kept at a comfortable sixty-eight degrees, that customs inspection occurred while he slept, and that the conductor, "an Englishman, by the way," was very polite. The writer enjoyed getting to know his fellow passengers and, most of all, he appreciated the food. He described as "simple and wholesome" the following lunch menu:

Hors d'œuvres varies
Filets de sole au vin blanc
Côtelettes de mouton, à la Mont Cenis
Petits pois à l'Anglaise
Galantine de volaille
Langue écarlate
Fromage
Fruits
Café et Liqueurs

He was traveling in November and said that the peas, which were fresh, had come from Brindisi, in the south of Italy. The pears at dessert were "the finest I have ever eaten, and the grapes were Chasselas—the real thing." The train route went through the Mont Cenis tunnel, which is why the mutton chops are described as "à la Mont Cenis." Galantine de volaille is a boned and rolled stuffed chicken usually served cold. So this was a dish that could have been prepared ahead of time, which would have been helpful since lunch was served shortly after the train left Calais. Similarly Langue écarlate is pickled tongue, another popular menu item of the time, and also served cold. The price of lunch was, he wrote, "just four shillings!" Later that afternoon, tea was served. When it was time for dinner, he and his fellow travelers, who included the editor of a London newspaper, a celebrated opera singer and his "charming wife," members of the Imperial House of Russia, and an attaché of the British Embassy in Rome, went to the restaurant car and enjoyed the following dinner:

Hors d'œuvres
Consommé à la Duchesse
Barbue, sauce Hollandaise
Aloyau de bœuf rôti
Haricots verts
Poulet de grains

Salades
Soufflé à la Rome Express
Glaces
Fromage, Dessert
Café, Liqueurs

This was typical of the fare the wealthy enjoyed elsewhere at the time. Consommé is infrequently served today, but in the late nineteenth and early twentieth centuries it appeared on dinner menus as often as turtle soup. It appears to be a simple broth; however, it is a complex dish. It's a broth, but a broth taken to the nth degree and a test of a cook's skill. Another contributor to the *Railway Magazine* called it the "infallible test" of a kitchen.[12] Consommé starts with a good stock. Then one adds a *raft* to the stock. A raft is a mixture of egg whites, ground meat, a *mirepoix* (finely chopped carrots, onions, and celery), and tomatoes along with herbs and spices. As the stock simmers, the mixture clusters together and rises to the surface of the broth like an island, or a raft, in the sea. The raft pulls out all the impurities that tend to cloud stock. Once it has done its work, it must be carefully skimmed off and discarded. The resulting consommé should be richly flavored and perfectly clear.

In 1913, the famed Belle Epoque caricaturist known as Sem tweaked the well-to-do as they dined aboard the Paris to Nice train. Courtesy of the Bridgeman Art Library

As time-consuming as consommé is to make, it can be made in large quantities, refrigerated, and reheated for service, an advantage in professional kitchens. Today, modernist cuisine methods simplify the clarification process. Perhaps they will make consommé popular again.

Cookbooks of the era include many different consommés. *Larousse Gastronomique* lists more than two dozen variations, from a cold consommé with truffles and port or sherry to consommé a l'impériale with poached cock's combs and kidneys, rice, peas, and finely shredded savory pancakes. It does not include an à la Duchesse variation. Other books do, but their descriptions vary. Some describe it as chicken stock served with tiny cheese profiteroles. Others say it has strips of white chicken meat added. Still others describe it as embellished with a julienne of chicken, tongue, and asparagus. The choice is up to the chef.

The fish on the menu is barbue (or brill) a large, flat fresh-water fish. In this instance it was served with hollandaise sauce. Aloyau de bœuf rôti is a roast sirloin of beef. The writer does not say where the green beans served at dinner came from, but presumably they were as fresh as the lunchtime peas. Poulet de grains is a corn-fed chicken, a term that sounds as if it came from a twenty-first-century menu but was typical on nineteenth-century ones.

The dinner cost just five shillings and sixpence, another bargain, according to the writer. With dinner, he and his companions shared "a bottle of light Bordeaux and a bottle of dry Imperial '84." He wrote, "Fear not, gentle reader, we were three—the Attaché, my friend the editor, and myself." A bottle of wine and a bottle of champagne for three people is a lot by today's standards, especially when we learn that after dinner they went to the smoking room and drank whiskey and soda while they played cards. However, it was not considered excessive at the time.

Breakfast was perfectly civilized. A waiter came to the writer's compartment in the morning and inquired as to whether he preferred coffee, tea, or chocolate. A few minutes later, the waiter returned and "a nice white serviette was spread on the little table in my compartment alongside my bed, and I was served with a delicious cup of *café au lait*, some toast, and a brioche."

The writer was clearly a man who cared about food and was always thinking about his next meal. As the train passed through the vineyards of the Piedmont and passed Asti, he noted, "I must have some of its Spumante with my lunch." When it went on to Alessandria, he wrote, "I will have a slice of its *salame crudo* with the *Asti Spumante*."

In addition to the typical menus of the time, the Wagons-Lits restaurant cars were known for serving the specialties of the various regions as they passed through them. At each stop, they picked up fresh produce, locally baked breads, wines of the region, and whatever else the local area provided for the enjoyment of their passengers. So the anonymous writer could be assured of enjoying the Spumante and salame crudo with his lunch.[13]

Pullman in England

While Nagelmackers was establishing his legendary Wagons-Lits Company on the continent, Pullman was expanding his company to England. In 1873, he entered into a contract with England's longest line, the Midland Railway Company, to provide the company with dining room, drawing room, and sleeping cars. The English were impressed with Pullman's sophisticated dark brown cars, since they were more modern and more elegant than existing English cars.

English railway passengers had coped with the lack of food on their railroads in various ways. Some packed their own lunches in a "Railway Companion," a container with a space for a sandwich, a flask, and a candle or oil reading lamp. The lamp was necessary because lighting in the compartments was so dim.[14] Some lines sold "Luncheon Baskets" that typically contained half a chicken, ham or tongue, salad, bread, and cheese along with a half bottle of claret for three shillings. A two-shilling basket contained veal and ham pie, salad, cheese, and bread with a bottle of stout. There were also one-shilling tea baskets containing tea, bread and butter, plum cake, and a chocolate bar. Although there were problems with keeping hot foods hot and returning the baskets to the correct stations, the refreshments baskets were popular. In his book, *Dining at Speed*, Chris de Winter Hebron suggests that the railroad companies liked them because they solved the problem of dining on the trains without necessitating buying, equipping, and staffing dining cars. Passengers liked the baskets because they had the festive air of picnics.[15]

Even after dining cars were introduced to England, they were not on every line. Writing about his childhood at the turn of the twentieth century, author Philip Unwin remembered traveling home from a Cornish holiday with his parents and siblings when they discovered to their chagrin that there was no restaurant car attached to their train. An understanding conductor promptly telegraphed to a station fifty miles ahead for tea baskets. When the train pulled in, a man was on the platform with baskets in hand. The baskets held a pot of freshly made tea, milk, bread and butter, Madeira cake, and jam. Unwin explained that the baskets were labeled "Yeovil Junction" so that after the empty baskets were turned in, they could be returned to the correct stations. Unwin wrote that it was "a most neat and tidy arrangement and typical of the times."[16]

In 1905, this luncheon basket, with its chicken, bread, cheese, pale ale, and implements was sold on London & North Western Railway trains for 3 shillings (15 pence), a day's pay for many railway workers. Copyright © National Railway Museum/Science & Society Picture Library

One of the most popular features Pullman brought to England was the lavatory. Previously, because lavatories were lacking on English lines, shops sold a rubber apparatus that gentlemen strapped on their legs under their trousers before a trip. The devices were known as "secret travelling lavatories."[17] Ladies simply had to do without until Pullman cars arrived on the scene.

The Pullman cars also offered a smoother ride, thanks to their six- or eight-wheel design. English cars typically had four wheels, which meant a bumpier ride. On a Pullman, famously, the ride was so smooth one's champagne didn't spill.

The first Pullman dining cars ran on the Great Northern Railway between Leeds and London in 1879. In his 1917 book *The Story of the Pullman Car*, Joseph Husband merely said the first meal served on the train consisted of "soups, fish, entrees, roast joints, puddings and fruits for dessert, a truly English bill of fare."[18]

When two new Pullman dining cars made an inaugural run from London's St. Pancras Station to Leicester and back in 1882, *The New York*

Times reprinted a *London News* article describing the trip. The *News* reporter called the dining cars "marvels of skill, taste, and ingenuity." The dining car woodwork was mahogany, and the fittings were, he wrote, "only a little less elaborate than those of the drawing room." Each dining car seated twenty at tables for two with comfortable high-backed seats. There was an electric bell at every table to call the waiter. At one end was a smoking room; at the other were the kitchen and a butler's pantry. Of the meal itself, he wrote "though it bore the name of a 'luncheon' it was in fact an excellent, well-cooked, and well-served dinner, the *menu* equaling that of a first-class hotel, and the ample courses being well appreciated by the travelers."[19]

Unfortunately, although he listed the names of all the notables who were on the inaugural run, he did not list the dishes. Presumably the menu was similar to the meals served on the Wagons-Lits cars or, as the writer said, at a first-class hotel.

Nagelmackers Celebrates

In 1898, Nagelmackers celebrated the twenty-fifth anniversary of the Wagons-Lits Company with a festive banquet at the Royal Conservatory of Music in Liège, the town where he was born. The company's trains brought prominent railway and government officials from all over Europe to Belgium for the grand occasion.

The banquet menu was illustrated with goddesses carrying flaming torches, the dates 1873–1898, the name Companie International des Wagons-Lits et Des Grands Express Européens, and the company crest. The dinner was equally grand. In addition to oysters and turtle soup, the menu included salmon trout à la Chambord—an elegant preparation of whole stuffed fish braised in red wine and garnished with such delicacies as fish quenelles, mushroom caps, and truffles shaped like olives.

There was also a saddle of venison, a *chaud-froid* of spiny lobster, and truffles with champagne. Colette once wrote that white wine did as well as champagne in this presentation, but for a Wagons-Lits anniversary, nothing but champagne would do. The menu also included parfait de foie gras. One of the most famous recipes for the dish originated with French chef Fernand Point. He marinated the *foie* in port, cognac, and nutmeg, studded it with truffles, and then poached it in chicken fat. Quite probably the Wagon-Lits version was similarly *parfait*.

Plombière impératrice was one of the desserts. An ice cream dish, *plombière* is typically made with almond milk and enhanced with whipped cream and candied fruits steeped in kirsch. Calling it *plombière impératrice*, or fit for an empress, meant it was especially rich.

The banquet's *pièce de résistance* was *glaces Wagons-Lits*, ice cream served in detailed replicas of Wagons-Lits Company carriages that had been molded from marzipan.

The Other Side of the Tracks

The average person couldn't afford to travel in the style Nagelmackers was celebrating and wouldn't expect such luxury. When those who could afford it found themselves on less exalted trains, they were not pleased. Occasionally they aired their complaints in print. Their accounts unwittingly reveal the difficulties endured by ordinary travelers.

In 1886, the Baroness de Stoeckl, who was related to the British royal family, summarized her trip to the Mediterranean by saying "one lived through it." The trip was not in the style to which she was accustomed. She was unhappy with everything from the lack of a dining car to the rudimentary sleeping arrangements. Although the seat pulled down to form a bed, there were no sheets or blankets and it cost a franc to rent a pillow. She said it was not safe to undress because there might be an accident. There was no lavatory on her train. She reported that "most people took with them a most useful domestic utensil, the emptying of which necessitated the frequent lowering of the window."

Because the train lacked a dining car, the baroness was forced to eat at a station buffet. Her description of the rush to eat at the station would have been familiar to scores of average travelers all over the world. "There was a wild rush for the buffet," she said, and wrote that she'd barely begun to eat before it was announced that the train was about to leave. She complained that the passengers had to run like maniacs to catch it. Her breakfast the next morning was not the lovely affair served on the Rome Express in 1897. It was a "chipped cup of coffee with a *croissant*, already moist from the overflow on the saucer . . . thrust though the window."[20]

Even when there was a dining car, the experience might not be up to the usual standards of a Pullman or Nagelmackers. There was a dining car on the Trans-Siberian Express when Dr. Francis E. Clark, an American, traveled across Russia from China in 1900. However, he said, "Pullman would scarcely own the diner as an offspring of his invention." It consisted of one long table seating twenty in the middle of the car with a bar at one end serving drinks and "some delicacies dear to the Russian heart like caviare [sic], sardines and other little fish." In his account of the trip, he wrote:

To be sure, one must get used to the greasy Siberian soup and to the chunks of tough stewed meat, which may be beef, mutton, or pork, one is never certain which. But travellers who choose to go across Siberia should not be squeamish, and to think of eating in a dining-car, however primitive, while whirling across the plains a little south of Kamchatka, is enough to kill the spirit of criticism in the most confirmed growler who ever went around the world.

Clark's description of the Trans-Siberian was very different from the train Nagelmackers was exhibiting at the Paris Exposition at the time, and Clark was well aware of the disparity between the two. He wrote:

The Paris Exposition has made famous the Siberian train *de luxe*, with its moving panorama, its terminal stations at St. Petersburg and Peking, and its dinners at seven francs per head. The newspaper correspondent, too, who has seen it only in his mind's eye, as he sat at his own cosey [sic] fireside rehashing second-hand descriptions of its magnificence, has done his share to advertise it, until the wondering world has an idea that it is a veritable Waldorf-Astoria on wheels. . . . We read of library-cars and bath-cars, gymnasium-cars where one can make a century run on a stationary bicycle, elegant dinners, barber-shops where passengers receive a free shave every morning, pianos, and other luxuries too numerous to mention. As a matter of fact, the Siberian train *de luxe*, at least as it started from Irkutsk on the 20th day of June, in the year of our Lord 1900, was a rather shabby vestibuled train of three sleepers, a diner, and a baggage-car. It was luxurious, indeed, compared with the fourth-class emigrant train on which we had been journeying, but it is still many degrees behind the best American trains. It should be remarked, however, that the best cars had been sent to Paris for the Exposition, and it is doubtless true that the train we took is somewhat below the average of the Siberian trains *de luxe*.[21]

Siberia in Paris

The 1900 Paris Exposition introduced many wonders to fairgoers, from the Eiffel Tower to the splendor of the Pont Alexandre III, from Ferris wheels to motion pictures with sound, from the opening of the Buffet de la Gare de Lyon (later known as Le Train Bleu) to the German penny-in-the-slot restaurant that was the forerunner to New York's automats.

One of the attractions was the moving panorama of the Siberian train *de luxe* that Clark referred to in his book. Nagelmackers had brought three seventy-foot long carriages with salons, dining cars, and sleeping cars to the Exposition. Visitors could simulate a two-week-long, Trans-Siberian trip by sitting in one of the elegant Wagons-Lits carriages and watching the scenery along the route for an hour. The views of Moscow, Beijing, and the Great

Visitors to the 1900 Universal Exhibition in Paris were impressed by the Trans-Siberian Railroad exhibit at the Russian pavilion. Courtesy of the Bridgeman Art Library

Wall of China were produced by four layers of objects and paintings that moved along a belt at different speeds. The first layer was made of sand and rocks; the next was a screen painted with shrubs and greenery; then there was a screen featuring more distant mountains, forests, and rivers. The final images were of the cities and landmarks along the actual train route. The panorama was housed in the Siberian section of the Exposition's Russian Pavilion.

Because more than 40,000,000 people attended the seven-month-long Exposition, it was a splendid opportunity for Nagelmackers to introduce his finest cars to a wide audience. Those who experienced the Trans-Siberian panorama would have been favorably impressed by its vision of luxury travel. Possibly some of them were inspired to book a trip. If they did, their experience was probably as rewarding as advertised. The growing pains of the early years of train travel were, with a few exceptions, in the past. The future looked golden.

Escoffier's Influence

At the beginning of the twentieth century, Charles Auguste Escoffier was the world's most famous chef. He cooked for the royal and the renowned and, in 1919, became the first cook to be awarded the French Legion of Honor. Long after his death in 1935, his work continued to influence kitchen organization and cuisine in restaurants and hotel dining rooms, on steamships and railway dining cars.

Dame Nellie Melba was the most renowned opera singer in the world during the same era. Like Escoffier, she was also a celebrity. A native of Australia, Melba sang at venues all over the world, from Covent Garden to La Scala and the Metropolitan Opera House. It's little wonder that Escoffier would create a dish in her honor.

In true Victorian style, this should be served as Escoffier did, in a swan carved from ice and surrounded with spun sugar.

∽ Pêche Melba

4 peaches
Raspberry puree, below
Pint of vanilla ice cream

Blanch the peaches in boiling water for a minute or two, remove and drain them. When they're cool enough to handle, peel and stone them and cut in half or in slices.

Scoop the ice cream into four dishes or bowls and arrange peaches on top of the ice cream. Pour over some of the raspberry puree and serve. ▄▄▄▄▄▄▄▄

∽ Raspberry Puree

2 pints fresh raspberries or 12 ounces frozen unsweetened raspberries, thawed
½ cup sugar
1 teaspoon lemon juice

Combine all ingredients in a saucepan and cook over medium heat, stirring occasionally. Bring the mixture to the boiling point and cook until it begins to thicken. Strain through a sieve, pressing down to get all the juice and leave only the seeds. Let cool. ▄▄▄▄▄▄▄▄

Escoffier's Waldorf Salad

The salad now generally derided as a gloopy sweet mayonnaise-laden mixture of celery, apples, and walnuts, originated at the posh New York Waldorf Hotel. A version can be found in Escoffier's famous *Le Guide Culinaire*. Escoffier made his with celeriac, rather than celery. He did dress it with mayonnaise, but he thinned the mayonnaise with aspic. As most of us do not have aspic in the refrigerator, the mayonnaise can be thinned with some lemon juice.

∾ *Waldorf Salad*

1 cup chopped apple
1 cup chopped celeriac
¼ cup chopped, toasted walnuts
¼ cup mayonnaise
1 tablespoon lemon juice
Salt and pepper to taste
Salad greens

Mix the apple, celeriac, and walnuts together. Add lemon juice to mayonnaise and toss lightly with the apple, celeriac, and walnuts. Season with salt and pepper. Serve atop salad greens.

CHAPTER 4

❧ ⌘ ❧

Transporting Restaurants

January 1, 1900, marked more than the first page of a new calendar, or the beginning of a year or a century. It ushered in the start of a new and more prosperous era. The times were changing.

Among the well-to-do, dress, décor, and dining all became more relaxed and less formal. No one had the time, or in many cases the servants, for ten-course dinners anymore. There was money to be made and there were places to go. Women had more freedom, and some were leaving service jobs like maid and housekeeper and going to work in offices as typists and stenographers.

In England, Queen Victoria's death in 1901 brought Edward VII and a very different and livelier sensibility to the throne and the country. The Edwardian era was characterized by speed and the beginnings of modernity. In the United States, Theodore Roosevelt assumed the presidency in 1901 after the assassination of William McKinley. Roosevelt, just forty-two when he took office, became the country's youngest president and one of the most energetic. It was a promising time. Wages were increasing and the workweek was decreasing; for many, it was five days long rather than six. Some workers now had paid vacations and holidays, so they were able to travel and eager to do so. Railroads were ready to welcome them.

At the beginning of the century, most trains had vestibules, electric lights, flush toilets, and central heat. The pot-bellied stove so many passengers had complained about was no more. Railroads were moving faster and traveling farther. They crisscrossed countries and continents. A 1902 article in the

This 1916 postcard shows fashionable dining and scenic views on a European train. Compliments of Kyri Claflin

National Geographic Magazine reported that the United States boasted nearly 200,000 miles of steam railways; Russia, nearly 35,000; the German Empire nearly 32,000; France, more than 26,000; India, 25,000; Great Britain and Ireland, 21,700; Italy, nearly 10,000. Trains were crossing Japan, China, and the Alps, and would soon cross the Andes.

One could travel by rail from Paris to Rome in just two days, from England to Italy in three. Traveling across the United States was not only faster than it had been, it cost less. Special expedition fares and less luxurious rail cars made cross-country travel more affordable than ever. As a result, families that had never even considered traveling for pleasure were now taking vacation trips.

The Kings Are Dead

Within a few years of the turn of the century, the three giants of railroad travel and dining were dead, and others were running the companies they had built.

George Pullman died in 1897, his reputation in tatters as a result of an ugly, prolonged labor dispute. After his death, Robert Todd Lincoln, son of the late president, headed the business. By then, the Pullman name had entered the popular lexicon. Compact suitcases, originally designed to fit under the seat in a Pullman car, are called Pullmans. Small efficiency kitchens in urban apartments are known as Pullmans. Bread baked in a lidded pan to keep its top flat so the loaves can be stacked efficiently is called a Pullman or sandwich loaf. The pan itself is known as a Pullman pan. Years after Pullman's death, during the Depression, men who were down on their luck hopped rides on railroad box cars they dubbed "side-door Pullmans." Pullman had succeeded in changing travel and creating a thriving business. His achievements as well as his flaws are part of railroad history. Charles Fryer, author of *British Pullman Trains*, put it well: "Pullman gave his name first to a coach, then to a train, and finally to a notion, that of relative comfort in contrast to relative austerity, *Sybaris* instead of *Sparta*."[1]

Fred Harvey, famed creator of Harvey Houses and employer of the Harvey Girls, died in 1901. By then, the chain he built had grown to include fifteen hotels, forty-seven restaurants, and catering on the ferries that crossed San Francisco Bay. Dining cars were running on train lines across the country and Harvey's company controlled thirty of them. His sons ran the company after their father died. The Harvey name continued to stand for high quality for many years.

A Playskool Pullman carriage toy from the 1930s. Compliments of Roz Cummins, photograph by Charlotte Holt

Teddy bears travel, sleep, and eat in style in this child's Pullman car toy. Compliments of Roz Cummins, photograph by Charlotte Holt

Georges Nagelmackers died in 1905. He had lived to see his dream of luxury European rail travel come true. Before he died, the *Orient Express* was running successfully—without transfers or ferries—between Paris and Constantinople. The *Calais Mediterranée Express*—later and more famously known as *Le Train Bleu*—was taking elite travelers to stylish vacation spots on the Riviera. Other lines traveled to St. Petersburg, Madrid, Lisbon, Vienna, and Athens in grand style. His vision was not limited to luxurious train travel. To make sure his passengers had sufficiently grand places to stay when they arrived, Nagelmackers had established eleven first-class hotels throughout Europe. Davison Dalziel, who had become the director of Wagon-Lits in 1893, ran the company after Nagelmackers's death. The name "Orient Express" still serves as a catchall phrase for deluxe travel, even among those who have never ridden anything but a commuter train.

Long Live the Trains

The railroad business had begun as the romantic quest of a few individuals. Long after their deaths, when shrewd businessmen ran the railways, passengers and would-be passengers kept the allure alive. It's no wonder people romanticized trains. During the early years of the twentieth century, trains epitomized the era. They were fast moving, modern, and technologically advanced. They represented a better, more dynamic future. People who seldom traveled could look to the railways and see possibilities. Some, like those who went west on the emigrant trains, rode the trains to a new life. Others took trains to new jobs in cities that were previously too far from their small hometowns. At the very least, trains took people to new vacation spots. Trains made passengers' worlds at once bigger and more accessible.

Accordingly, Sunday newspapers introduced travel sections containing practical, service-oriented articles rather than the sophisticated compositions that appeared in magazines such as the *Atlantic Monthly*. To increase ridership, the Southern Pacific Railway introduced *Sunset* magazine in 1898, with articles about the attractions of the region served by its line, like the Yosemite Valley and the Santa Cruz shoreline. Its primary market was tourists rather than those who already lived in the West. Initially, the magazine did not carry advertising for the railroad and was distributed free at hotels and train stations. Before long, however, ads ran and paid subscriptions were available.[2]

Most railroad companies published guidebooks with descriptions of the sights passengers would see from the windows of their train as well as those that awaited at the destination. Tourists could also avail themselves of the many new travel books that described exotic sights, listed hotels and restaurants, and included maps. Timetables, posters, ads, and promotional brochures all helped build tourism and increase railroad revenues. Often, travelers themselves published books documenting their experiences, many with photographs of the most scenic areas. There was no lack of information or inspiration for those who yearned to get away.

For many passengers, the dining car was a train's main attribute. They saw trains largely as transporting restaurants. A writer identified only by the initials T.F.R. said he had traveled the world in everything from "a bicycle to a balloon, but there is no mode of journeying that appeals more strongly to my imagination and innate sense of *bienêtre* than the restaurant-car attached to an express train." T.F.R. said he took a trip from London to Ipswich, a distance of seventy-five miles, solely to enjoy dinner in the dining car and stave off his "ennui." His article, titled "The Pleasures of the Dining-Car," in a 1900 edition of the *Railway Magazine*, recommended the practice:

> It is so odd to be speeding along at fifty or sixty miles an hour, shooting tunnels, leaping rivers, flying through the heart of smiling pasture land, or flashing through great centres of commercial industry—ever annihilating space,

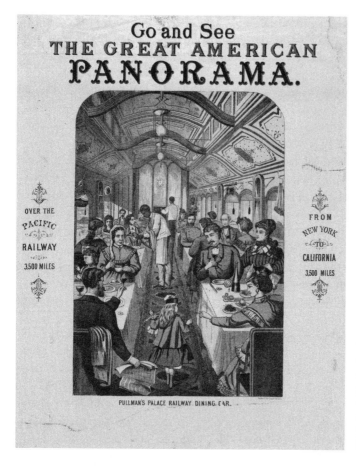

The best way to see America was from a train, preferably one with a fine dining car. Courtesy of the Wisconsin Historical Society

bridging remote distances, and all the while to be comfortably enjoying your mayonnaise of salmon, picking the leg of a grouse to the accompaniment of a glass of good burgundy, or a still more fascinating sparkling beverage. . . . It is exhilarating to a degree this style of locomotion, and for putting the clock back—for the suspension of time—there is nothing like it on earth.[3]

Many years later and miles away, in the 1940s, a group of Texans formed the habit of enjoying their Sunday dinner aboard the *Katy Limited* on the Missouri-Kansas-Texas Railroad. They went to church in San Antonio, and then took the train to Austin, some eighty-three miles away, to have dinner in the dining car. After they ate, they took the 3:20 *Texas Special* back to San Antonio.[4]

Even people who seldom traveled were fans of railroads and everything associated with them. Those who lived in the country recall going to the local train station when they were young, just to watch trains pass by as they dreamed of the places they would visit one day. They wistfully remember the sound of the shrill whistle of a train huffing down the tracks.

New Yorkers of a certain age still talk about visiting Grand Central Station as youngsters simply to wander about the splendid station and watch trains come and go. Some, who never traveled on name trains like the *20th Century Limited*, recall visiting the station when young and managing to persuade the station guards to let them walk on the famous red carpet that led to the train. Many people recall the grandeur of New York's Pennsylvania Station lovingly and rue its demolition.

Trains in Song and Story

Almost from their inception, trains have inspired writers, artists, composers, and choreographers. The Lumière brothers' silent film, *L'arrivée d'un train à La Ciotat*, consisted simply of a steam locomotive pulling into a station in the town of La Ciotat and was just fifty seconds long. Yet at its Paris premiere in 1896 the audience was amazed and astonished by it. Ever since, trains have been featured in countless films, some illustrating the splendors of first-class travel; others, such as the excellent 1980 BBC drama "Caught on a Train," showing the dreary, crowded conditions more passengers experienced and the unsettling encounters that might take place in a crowded compartment.

One of the best train films is the MGM Technicolor musical, *The Harvey Girls*, starring Judy Garland, Ray Bolger, and Angela Lansbury. Released in 1946, the film featured Johnny Mercer's song "The Atchison, Topeka & the Santa Fe" (Mercer added *the* before Santa Fe because it sounded better musically). The film and the song were both huge hits. Ironically, the railroad had fallen on hard times by then, and according to Stephen Fried, author of *Appetite for America*, the song made more money that year than the Santa Fe Railroad did.[5]

Over the years, songwriters immortalized trains with a nearly endless list of songs, upbeat ones like "Chattanooga Choo Choo" and "Wabash Cannonball," and sorrowful ones such as "Brother Can You Spare a Dime," about the men who built the railroads and were suffering in the Depression.

In 1900, a train enthusiast named Joshua Lionel Cowen founded a company that made model trains. As a result, he turned children into train enthusiasts. For years afterwards, a set of Lionel trains was the most wished-for gift for boys, and some girls, all over the United States. As they set up and played with their model trains, they could imagine traveling on the real thing when they grew up. Many parents bought the train sets as much for themselves as for their children.

Children's books such as *The Little Engine That Could*, *Thomas the Tank Engine*, *The Boxcar Children*, and *The Polar Express* also turned youngsters into train fans. Paddington Bear, a beloved character in English children's literature, was named after the London railway station. One of the more famous trains in contemporary children's (and grown-ups') books is, of course, Harry Potter's *Hogwarts Express*.

Adult novels with trains as a setting are legion. Authors from Anthony Trollope and Charles Dickens and, in more recent times, Michael Crichton and Paul Theroux have set stories on trains. But no one had more impact on the romance of the railroad than the incomparable Agatha Christie with

The most famous train mystery of them all: *Murder on the Orient Express.* Courtesy of the Bridgeman Art Library

her books and subsequent films and television shows featuring trains. *Murder on the Orient Express* is the most famous; but she also wrote *The Mystery of the Blue Train, The ABC Murders, 4.50 From Paddington,* and *The Girl in the Train.* The fact that murders regularly took place on or near Christie's trains did not dampen railways fans' enthusiasm for train travel.

First-Class Travel

For those who could afford first-class travel at the turn of the twentieth century, trains were enclosed, bubble-like places where they could escape everyday considerations. As passengers sped along from Paris to Nice or New York to Chicago, they enjoyed exquisite service, fine dining, and the company of friends, or at least people with whom they felt comfortable.

Lucius Beebe, one of the most enthusiastic train aficionados, described the allure of train travel when he wrote, "A ride on the steamcars was a glorious adventure in a fairyland where there were cherubs painted on the ceilings and both terrapin and Porterhouse on the dollar dinner."[6]

Porters, valets, and maids tended to the passengers' every need. On long trips, passengers could sleep comfortably in a bed with fresh linens and enjoy breakfast delivered to their compartments in the morning. If that weren't enough, some passengers on the Wagons-Lits sleepers had their maids put silk sheets over the regular linens.

Ladies could bathe, have a manicure, relax with a massage, and have their hair done. Men could shower, be shaved, and have their shoes shined. Stock market reports and the morning newspapers were available, if passengers wanted to let the world intrude for a few moments. Or they could repair to the smoking room and enjoy a card game. Or go to the observation car and settle down with a book or magazine from its library. Best of all, they could look forward to a delectable dinner with perhaps a cocktail at the bar first.

First-Class Dining

Dining car menus at the turn of the twentieth century were becoming simpler than in years earlier, but were no less elegant. Some regional specialties continued to be served. The Englishman on the *Rome Express* could have his salame crudo and Asti Spumante when passing through northern Italy. Passengers on the Canadian Pacific Railways train that ran between Montreal and Vancouver enjoyed Nova Scotia salmon and British Columbia peaches. Chicken pie was a specialty of the Great Northern Railway, on its long route from Minnesota to Washington State. In its ads, the railway claimed it was

The London & North Eastern Railway's perky chef promised dining perfection. Copyright © National Railway Museum/Science & Society Picture Library

made with "plenty of chicken (bones omitted), potatoes, thick, rich chicken roux and—here's the secret—Bacon Crisps."[7]

Apart from such specialties, though, dining car menus had become strikingly similar to each other, as well as to those on oceangoing steam ships, hotels, and fine dining restaurants. Wherever the well-to-do traveled, Escoffier's international style dominated. Upper-class travelers scoffed at the plebeian Cook's Tours for their conformity and predictability, for their roast beef and pudding Englishness, but elite travel was just as uniform and homogenous in its own way. With the exception of a few intrepid adventurers, the well-to-do sailed on the same ships, rode the same railways, stayed at the same hotels, associated with the same people, and ate the same foods wherever they went, from New York to Nice, from Genoa to Geneva.[8]

From consommé to spring lamb with mint sauce to pudding, the dishes served on the Red Star Line steamship S.S. *Zeeland* sailing from Antwerp to New York in 1905 are twins to those served on Pullman and Wagons-Lits dining cars of the same time. Even in Japan, where one would expect to dine very differently, menus in the hotels Westerners frequented were similar to those in Europe. In 1886, George Moerlein of Cincinnati, Ohio, whose family owned the Christian Moerlein Brewing Company, set off on a trip around the world. When Moerlein arrived in Yokohama, he went immediately to the Grand Hotel. Located in the Bund area where the buildings were largely owned and operated by Europeans, the hotel, Moerlein wrote in *A Trip Around the World*, "has the reputation of setting the best table in the Far-East."

The hotel's owners were French, were trained as professional cooks, and served the best of everything, according to Moerlein. Although the portions were small, "an order could be duplicated as many times as the guest wished," he explained. "You could not help relishing the food," he said, and the service was first class. The Japanese waiters wore "tight black leggings and short jackets" and with their great skill in handling dishes, they were "a pleasure to behold." Because the waiters did not speak English, the guests ordered by number. He reproduced the menu in his account of his trip to "give the reader an idea of the meals served and how."

GRAND HOTEL

J. Boyer & Co., ---------- Proprietors

DINNER. —Bill of Fare.
Yokohama, January 17th, 1886.
[1] Swallow's Nest Soup
[2] Fish a la Chambord
ENTREES
[3] Loin of Veal a la Polonaise
[4] Snipe a l'Imperiale
[5] Boiled Mutton a la Reine
VEGETABLES
[6] Beans [7] Spinach
[8] Carrots [9] Salsifis
JOINTS
[10] Roast Beef [11] Roast Truffled Capons
[12] Curry and Rice

ENTREMENTS
[13] Pudding a la DuBarry
[14] Choux Pralines aux Violettes
[15] Sorbets Riches
[16] Coffee. [17] Tea.[9]

In 1912, the Japanese Travel Bureau was formed to encourage tourism. The organization was comprised of representatives of government and railway, hotel, and steamship companies, and encouraged the establishment of European-style restaurants in Japan. The goal was to make tourists feel comfortable by providing them with Western-style menus, cutlery, tables, and chairs. In other words, to take the foreignness out of foreign travel. Judging by the menu at the Grand Hotel, the goal had already been met.

Menus nearly everywhere were comparable. Most offered oysters—raw on the half shell, broiled, creamed, fricasseed, roasted, fried, pickled, as a cocktail, in chowder, and in fritters. Often they were specifically identified by their point of origin as Blue Points, Wellfleets, Cotuits, Shrewsburys, and others. Along with the oysters, menus continued to feature consommé and turtle soup. Relishes included chow chow, olives, radishes, celery, and nuts.

A fish course was generally served. Popular fish included everything from crab to lobster, from trout to bluefish, from mackerel to smelts. Everything, that is, except tuna. In the United States, fresh tuna was a game fish. It was an exciting catch for sportsmen who reveled in reeling in a 100–200-pound tuna, having their picture taken with it, and possibly seeing it reported in the local newspaper. Their enthusiasm was not enough for them to actually eat the tuna. In fact, in 1901, when the sports fishermen of the Tuna Club of Santa Catalina, California, held their annual banquet, the men feasted on little neck clams, abalone, fried plaice, and other dishes. Tuna was not on the menu.[10]

Few Americans ate tuna at the time. Immigrants from Japan or Italy were used to it and enjoyed it when it was available. But it wasn't until canners learned how to steam tuna so it was whiter and less oily that many Americans tried it. By 1912, when it was marketed as "Chicken of the Sea," it began to catch on and by 1918 canned tuna was one of the most popular fish in the country. Finally, in the 1960s, fresh tuna made it onto the American dinner plate.[11]

At the beginning of the century, mutton continued to be popular, whether saddle, chop, kidney, or roasted leg. Lamb, though not served as frequently, was becoming more widespread and by the 1920s, it began to overtake mutton. Roast beef was always popular. Tongue was frequently served cold and pickled. Every sort of duck—canvasback, teal, mallard, ruddy—was served, as well as game birds such as grouse and pheasant. However, as game was becoming scarcer, regulations were beginning to limit its availability.

Vegetables including potatoes, peas, asparagus, beets, cauliflower, eggplant, and spinach were all typical menu choices, along with salads often titled "dressed lettuce." Saratoga chips, now more commonly known as potato chips, burst on the scene in the 1880s and quickly became widespread. On menus of the era, potato salad was called "potato mayonnaise." Ice cream, apple pie, cakes, puddings, baked Alaska, charlotte russe, and soufflés were characteristic desserts everywhere.

A cheese course was frequently served after dessert and usually included Stilton, Roquefort, Gorgonzola, Camembert, or varieties of cheddar. In the United States, Bent's water crackers, listed by name, accompanied the cheeses. An early branding success, the company, founded in 1801, is still in business in the town of Milton, near Boston, Massachusetts.

There was a plethora of potables in the early twentieth century. Wine accompanied most meals and wine lists were extensive. They nearly always included champagne and Madeira as well as claret, Rhine wine, port, and Burgundy. Rail aficionado Beebe said that the appropriate breakfast wines were hock (a Briticism for white German wine), claret, and champagne. There seemed to be no time, place, or occasion when champagne was not appropriate.

A wide variety of beers and ales, often locally brewed, were served. After-dinner spirits were likely to include bitters, crème de menthe, cognac, and chartreuse. Drinks such as the sherry cobbler, the crusta, and brandy, whiskey, or gin cocktails had been popular since the Civil War era. By the turn of the century, barmen had expanded their repertoire to include the gin fizz, whiskey sour, Tom Collins, and the Manhattan, as well as the martini, the drink H.L. Mencken called "the only American invention as perfect as the sonnet."[12]

Private Varnish

From the earliest days of rail travel, queens, kings, and presidents traveled in private cars for reasons of privacy and security. Private cars also gave them an added measure of comfort in an era when train travel was far from luxurious. Almost immediately, other passengers arranged to set themselves apart as well. Lucius Beebe reported that in 1834 a group of businessmen paid the Boston & Providence Railroad fifteen dollars a day to reserve their own coach car for their daily commute to Boston from Dedham and back.

The distance is a mere twenty-one miles, and fifteen dollars was a considerable sum at the time. Beebe called the coach "the first club car" and said, facetiously, there was no record that a bar on the train was stocked with "Medford rum or that cards were played en route."[13]

When Pullman and others began producing elegant, comfortable rail cars, the finest of them, painted and polished to gleaming perfection, were called *varnish* trains. The luxury or varnish trains were, as Pullman had promised, the equivalent of the best hotels on rails. From the late nineteenth to the early twentieth centuries, they offered passengers everything from exquisite meals to impeccable service, but all that was not enough for some. To distinguish themselves even further, some members of the upper class bought their own railroad cars. Private varnish was finer than the finest. It was the ultimate status symbol.

Anyone who was anyone, from tycoons to socialites to celebrities, traveled in private varnish and dined in style. J.P. Morgan hired Louis Sherry, the renowned New York caterer to the Gilded Age's 400, to supervise his menus when Morgan traveled across the country. Financier Collis P. Huntington's private car *Oneonta* boasted a wine cellar few private homes could match. The Turkish-American investor James Ben Ali Haggin hired a French chef from Foyot in Paris for his car, *Salvator,* and was said to dine on a gold dinner service. The Princess Vilma Lwoff-Parlaghy of Hungary traveled in a private car supplied by the New York, New Haven & Hartford Railroad when she was in America. She had her lunch served on her own gold plates.[14] Lillie Langtry, who was more famous for her love affairs than her theatrical talent, owned a car where she dined on quail and tenderloin steaks prepared by a French chef.[15]

Some private cars were owned by railway executives and could be considered company or business cars. However, the early twentieth century was not an era of executive accountability. If the Busch family of St. Louis had beer piped under pressure to all the compartments of the *Adolphus* as Beebe claimed, that was their privilege. Executives' expenses were considered to be no one's business as long as profits were up and stockholders were happy. When a private car was owned by a railroad company and dubbed the business car of its president, he might or might not ever conduct business in the car. Beebe, an unabashed fan of private varnish whether it was the property of a private person or a business, wrote: "Some of the most sumptuously appointed private cars in the record were those of railroad presidents who stoutly maintained that they were no more than frugal conveyances for the transaction of the company's business."[16]

Beebe was one of the very last owners of private varnish cars who made no pretense of his cars being anything but grand pleasure vehicles. Born in 1902,

Beebe, who died in 1966, lived his life as a dapper, sophisticated Edwardian despite—or because of—the fact that he came of age in a later era; one that was less congenial to his taste. The phrase *bon vivant* was used to describe him so often that it might have been mistaken for his first name. Beebe was born into a wealthy Boston area family, but he was anything but a proper Bostonian if that term means sedate, stuffy, and conventional. He was expelled from Yale. Rumor had it that he kept a roulette wheel and a bar in his dorm. Subsequently, he went to Harvard, then became a well-known society writer in New York. The author of *The Stork Club Bar Book*, he found his great subject in railroad lore and legend, describing the golden years when railways were at their zenith. He wrote or cowrote more than a dozen railroad books, many of which featured his own photography, and he did more than anyone to keep the romance of railroading alive.

Beebe wrote about all kinds of railroad cars, but he was most enamored with private varnish. In *Mr. Pullman's Elegant Palace Car*, published in 1961, after the era had ended, he wrote:

> Its possession combined luxurious convenience with the romantic hold railroading had for the popular imagination and the combination exalted it above ownership of the Hope Diamond. . . . Swimming pools were for successful greengrocers and electrical contractors. Palm Beach and charge accounts at Cartier were for well-placed stockbrokers. The private Pullman, its dark green varnish and brass-railed observation platform headed for Florida or Del Monte or the Adirondacks, was for grand seigneurs and the feudal overlords of the American economy.[17]

Beebe rationalized the expense by saying that a private railroad car cost less than a chateau on Nob Hill. While the chateau might cost $3,000,000, a private railroad car could be built for between $50,000 and $250,000. He believed that was a great bargain. While such cost might not be extravagant in Beebe's world, he failed to mention details like the other expenses associated with private varnish ownership. The fees to be paid to the railroad when the car and its owners were traveling, storage costs when it was parked in a rail yard between trips, furnishings for the car, its upkeep, and its staffing all added up as well.

Generally, a private car consisted of a dining room seating eight to ten people, an observation salon where one could relax and enjoy the passing scenery, a master stateroom with a bath, three or four guest staterooms, a fully equipped galley with storage space, ice boxes, and linen closet, and quarters for the crew. The size of the spaces varied according to the owner's needs and wishes. The car could be built with a larger dining area, more or fewer guest rooms, or a larger or smaller master stateroom. The car could be whatever its owner desired.

Special appointments like Italian marble bathtubs, wood-burning fireplaces, libraries, and wine cellars were up to the owner to choose. Naturally, private car owners traveled with their own chefs and servers. Some also employed English butlers and footmen in full livery, as well as other servants. On some private cars, guests dressed for dinner just as they would on an ocean liner or at their own home.

Food costs were, no doubt, considerable since the owners ate in a style some might call extravagant. Jay Gould, the notorious nineteenth-century financier and railroad baron, believed himself to have a delicate stomach and restricted his diet to milk, ladyfingers, and champagne. He traveled with his private pastry chef who was expected to bake the ladyfingers fresh daily. Of course, there was always plenty of champagne on ice. To make sure he had not only fresh milk, but also the right kind of milk available at all times, he kept a cow in the baggage car of the train that carried his private car. This was not just any cow. It was a particular cow whose milk contained the amount of butterfat that Gould believed agreed with him.

Private cars and personal chefs meant that the owners and their guests were not limited to a set menu. They could arrange for anything they wanted, whenever they wanted it, from caviar sandwiches to French pastry. On the other hand, if they wanted to dine on the simple foods their mother or grandmother made rather than international cuisine, they could have that as well.

Self-indulgence was the rule on the private cars, not the exception. One private car owner, a mushroom lover, had a miniature mushroom cellar mounted under his car, according to Beebe. The story is difficult to believe. But whether it is true or not, it does show the extremes to which some of the wealthy might have gone to satisfy their whims, and the desire of others to revel in the fables and the foibles of the rich.

A Private Car Chef

Rufus Estes began his life as a slave and ultimately became a well-known and highly regarded private chef and author. He was born in 1857 in Tennessee, the youngest of nine children. At the start of the Civil War, he wrote, "all the male slaves in the neighborhood for miles around ran off and joined the 'Yankees.' This left us little folks to bear the burdens." When he was just five years old, he had to haul water, take care of cows, and do many other farm chores. After the war and freedom, he worked at odd jobs until, at sixteen, he went to work at a restaurant. He must have learned to be an excellent cook,

Rufus Estes' Good Things to Eat
The First Cookbook by an African-American Chef

Rufus Estes, a former slave, became a private dining car chef and author. Courtesy of Dover Publications

for he was hired by Pullman and put in charge of a dining car that catered to the most important passengers when he was twenty-six. He cooked for the renowned explorer Sir Henry Morton Stanley, for presidents Benjamin Harrison and Grover Cleveland, for famed singer Adelina Patti, and for Princess Eulalie of Spain.

In 1894, Estes set sail for Tokyo as private chef to Mr. and Mrs. Nathan A. Baldwin on their voyage to view the cherry blossom festival. When he returned to the United States, he took charge of the $20,000 private rail car of Arthur Stilwell, the millionaire railroad entrepreneur and inventor of the Stilwell Oyster Car.

In 1907, Estes became the chef of the Chicago Subsidiary Companies of United States Steel Corporation. His book, *Good Things to Eat*, was published in 1911, and reprinted in 1999. In his foreword, he calls the book the child of his "brain and experience," and says he hopes his dishes will "with equal grace, adorn the home table or banquet board."[18]

Estes's recipes include everything from breakfast dishes to desserts, from game birds to gumbo, from pigs' feet to parfaits. Many are everyday dishes while others are perfectly suited to festive occasions. The book includes many of the dishes commonly associated with international fine dining. It has recipes for oysters, bisques, roasts, steaks served with maître d'hôtel butter, and soufflés. Estes also included traditional Southern dishes, some simple casseroles, and even vegetarian dishes, which no doubt reflected the preferences of his clients.

Surprisingly, Good Things to Eat does not have a recipe for consommé, that mainstay of elite dining. It does have many recipes for other soups, including bisques of lobster, clam, and oyster. There is a recipe for meatballs for turtle soup, but no recipe for turtle soup itself. The meatballs are made from turtle flesh, fried, and then added to the hot soup. The recipe is listed under the heading "Lenten Dishes." Turtles could be eaten during Lent when meat was forbidden as they were considered to be fish. However, Estes also lists quenelles made variously of chicken, calves' liver, and beef marrow as Lenten dishes. His was a very liberal interpretation of Lenten rules.

"White Soup" is Estes's most elegant soup. It is made with meat stock, grated French rolls, almonds, and cream cooked and then strained through a silk sieve to a velvety smoothness. The soup dates back at least to seventeenth-century France and La Varenne, the author of Le Cuisinier François, who called it Potage à la Reine, or Queen's Soup. Jane Austen fans may remember the scene in Pride and Prejudice when Mr. Bingley says they'll schedule the Netherfield ball as soon as his cook has made enough white soup. Recipes vary over the years, but it is always considered an elegant soup, one fit for a queen. Or a twentieth-century railroad baron.

Estes shared the era's love of organ meats. His book has recipes for broiled sheep's kidneys, calves or sheep's tongues, sheep's brains, and other such dishes. Recipes like Brunswick stew, Southern corncake, and hickory nut cake reveal a Southern influence. Estes wrote that he sweetened his sweet potatoes because it "pleases the Southern taste, which demands sugar added to the naturally sweet vegetable."[19]

It is possible that one of Estes's clients or someone his clients entertained was a vegetarian because Estes included several recipes made with nut meal or chopped nuts in lieu of meat. His "Peanut Meatose" is a mixture of corn-starch, tomato juice, peanut butter, and salt, poured into a can and steamed for four or five hours. There are also recipes for nut hash, a baked vegetable and nut casserole, a walnut loaf, and a nut and parsnip stew. These were all typical vegetarian dishes of the era.[20]

The biggest surprise in *Good Things to Eat* is its frugality. For a private chef working for the rich, the famous, and the fussy during the Gilded Age, Estes created exceptionally cost-conscious recipes. Was he trying to appeal to a wider audience than his private varnish clients? Or did he use these cost-cutting techniques on the private cars? Or were they included to broaden his audience to include ordinary cooks?

In the section he titles "Hints to Kitchen Maids," he recommended using the remains of yesterday's dinner to make today's lunch.[21] He used leftover meat in hashes, casseroles, and ragouts or stews. He noted that "inferior portions [of meat] such as the neck can be utilized in a curry." The recipe titled "Remnants of Ham with Peas" uses leftover ham chopped and mixed with canned peas and a white sauce, topped with breadcrumbs and baked.[22] He described his recipe for a beef ragout as "another way to serve the remnants of cold meat."[23] He patted leftover mashed potatoes into cakes and fried them. He described "Aunt Amy's Cake," as "a good cake and one which is also inexpensive in baking."[24] In these recipes, Estes sounds more like a frugal homemaker than a private chef.

But then there are his more lavish dishes. In one, Estes stuffed a turkey with three or four pounds of truffles.[25] They were not as expensive then as they are today, but truffles were still a luxury item at the time, and three or four pounds was an extravagance of truffles.

Presentation was important to Estes. His whimsical "Birds Nest Salad" calls for leaves of lettuce to "make a dainty little nest for each person." He tucked tiny speckled eggs made from cream cheese rolled in chopped parsley into the lettuce leaves. He recommended serving the salads with French dressing "hidden under the leaves of lettuce." He served various vegetable, chicken, or fish salads in baskets made from blanched, skinned, and seeded whole tomatoes. Before serving, he fashioned handles for the baskets from sprigs of watercress.[26]

One of his most elaborate dishes is called "Marbled Chicken." To make it, Estes separated the white and dark meat, chopped it, and pressed it into a mold in alternating layers. Then he poured chicken stock over it. After chilling and unmolding it, he cut the "Marbled Chicken" into thin slices that looked striped, or marbled, and served them garnished with watercress and sliced lemon.[27]

Estes's desserts shine. Puddings were among the era's most popular desserts, and the book has recipes for more than a dozen, from apple to Indian, along with the sauces to go with them. There are countless pies, pastries, soufflés, cakes, frostings, fillings, and many ice creams, including an unusual black currant ice cream garnished with crystallized cherries and leaves of angelica. Estes said his cranberry sherbet was often served at Thanksgiving dinner "after the roast." In a recipe for candied violets, he wrote, "Gather the required quantity of perfect sweet violets, white or blue. If possible pick in the early morning while the dew is still on them."[28]

When he wrote *Good Things to Eat*, Estes gave future generations an excellent collection of recipes. Whether it was his intention or not, he also provided a window into the era's tastes.

The early years of the twentieth century were a golden era for railroads and their passengers. Train travel had become as fast and fashionable as the times. The wealthy traveled and dined in unparalleled style, and ordinary folk could finally travel in comfort if not in luxury. The future seemed limitless. World War I, the Depression and, almost as serious for railroads, the development of air travel and automobiles were all too far on the horizon to be seen clearly.

Starting with Soup

In the late nineteenth and early twentieth centuries, most restaurant, hotel, and railroad dining car menus started with a selection of soups. They ranged from consommé to turtle, from bouillon to creamed vegetable to clam or oyster chowder. It seemed a meal wasn't a meal without a soup.

White soup was one of the most esteemed. Under various names, it had a long, illustrious past. Often called Queen's Soup, its first printed recipe was from famed French cook and author François Pierre La Varenne's *Le Cuisinier François*, published in Paris in 1651. After it was translated into English, versions of the recipe appeared in cookbooks in England and in the United States. It was basically a rich broth, which was strained and then enriched with almonds, breadcrumbs, and cream or milk. Sometimes eggs were added. Often small bread rolls were used as a garnish. When the rolls were stuck with almonds, it was called hedgehog soup. La Varenne garnished his with pomegranate seeds and pistachios and toasted its surface with a hot fire shovel. A salamander or, today, a cook's blowtorch would serve the same purpose.

This recipe comes from the cookbook published by private Pullman car chef Rufus Estes in *Good Things to Eat* (1911).

๑৴ White Soup

Put 6 pounds of lean gravy beef into a saucepan, with ½ gallon of water and stew gently until all the good is extracted and remove beef. Add to the liquor 6 pounds of knuckle of veal, ¼ pound ham, 4 onions, 4 heads of celery, cut into small pieces, a few peppercorns and a bunch of sweet herbs. Stew gently for seven or eight hours, skimming off the fat as it rises to the top. Mix with the crumbs of two French rolls, 2 ounces of blanched sweet almonds, and put in a saucepan with a pint of cream and a little stock, boil ten minutes, then pass through a silk sieve, using a wooden spoon in the process. Mix the cream and almonds with the soup, turn into a tureen, and serve.

Nineteenth-Century Drinks

In the United States before Prohibition struck in 1920, bartenders had a vast repertoire of drinks. One of the most popular was a drink known as Sherry Cobbler. The basic cobbler was made with a liquor shaken up with sugar, citrus fruit, and lots of ice. It was garnished with more fruit or berries and served with a straw. There were many different cobbler drinks—whiskey, rum, champagne—but the Sherry Cobbler was the hands-down favorite. Americans loved the drink. In fact, bold ladies ordered it at ice cream shops, instead of the much more proper dish of ice cream. England fell for the drink after Dickens character Martin Chuzzlewit praised it in the novel that bore the same name.

This recipe is from Jerry Thomas, the nineteenth century's most famous American bartender. He didn't specify the type of sherry. I used oloroso and skipped the sugar.

๑৴ Sherry Cobbler

(Use large bar glass.)
1 tablespoonful fine white sugar.
1 slice orange, cut into quarters.
2 small pieces pineapple.

Fill the glass nearly full of shaved ice, then fill it up with sherry wine. Shake up, ornament the top with berries in season, and serve with a straw. —Jerry Thomas, *How to Mix Drinks, or The Bon-Vivant's Companion.*

Thomas also wrote about the drink called a *crusta* and called it "an improvement on the 'cocktail.'" Crustas could be made with brandy, gin, or whiskey. The main feature that sets them apart from cocktails is that a wide strip of lemon peel is wrapped around the inside of the glass before the drink mixture is poured in. The peel adds flavor—as well as panache—to the drink. However, it is a bit tricky to drink without the peel slip-sliding away. Some mixologists have revived the crusta recently as they bring back the best of the vintage drinks. This is Jerry Thomas's recipe.

∾ Crusta

> 3 or 4 dashes gum syrup
> 2 do. bitters (Bogart's) [do = ditto]
> 1 wine glass brandy
> 1 or 2 dashes Curaçoa

Squeeze lemon peel; fill one-third full of ice, and stir with a spoon.

(Use small bar glass.)

The whiskey and gin crustas are made the same as the brandy crusta, using whiskey or gin instead of brandy.

Crusta is made the same as a fancy cocktail, with a little lemon juice and a small lump of ice added. First, mix the ingredients in a small tumbler, then take a fancy red wine glass, rub a sliced lemon around the rim of the same, and dip it in pulverized white sugar, so that the sugar will adhere to the edge of the glass. Pare half a lemon the same as you would an apple (all in one piece) so that the paring will fit in the wine glass, as shown in the cut, and strain the crusta from the tumbler into it.

Then smile. —Jerry Thomas, *How to Mix Drinks, or The Bon Vivant's Companion*

ଚ୍ଚ *Today's Crusta*

Yields: 2 servings

Lemon
Sugar

3 ounces Brandy
1 ounce orange Curaçoa
Dash of bitters
½ ounce lemon juice

Run a lemon wedge around the edge of the glasses, then dip them in a little sugar to coat the rim. Peel the lemon with a vegetable peeler to get a wide strip, then wrap it around the inside of the glass.

Mix the other ingredients in a chilled shaker with some ice, shake well, and pour carefully into the glasses. Try not to disturb the lemon peel.

Then, as Jerry Thomas said, smile.

CHAPTER 5

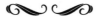

Streamlined Dining

On the morning of November 11, 1918, Pullman car 2419-D became the most famous dining car in Europe. Its fame came not from meals that had been served onboard. Nor did it come from its lavish décor or the exemplary service of its crew. Rather, the car was the setting for the end of World War I hostilities. That morning, representatives of the French, English, and German governments met in the dining car and signed the armistice to end the war that was supposed to end all wars.

Car 2419 had been converted into an office for Marshall Ferdinand Foch, the commander of the Allied forces, and was part of his mobile headquarters in the Compiegne Forest, about forty miles north of Paris. There the Germans conceded defeat, and the Allies declared their victory. Later, the official peace treaty was signed at Versailles. After the war, a granite monument and a structure to house the dining car were erected at the Compiegne site. For years, veterans of the war stood guard over the monument and the dining car, and visitors came from throughout the world to pay their respects.

During World War II, in 1940, an armistice between France and Germany was signed in car 2419. This time the Germans were victorious. After Hitler signed the armistice, he sent the car to Germany and had it displayed beside the Brandenburg Gate. Then the Germans destroyed the memorial in the forest. Nothing was left but the damaged railroad tracks. Shortly before the war actually ended, defeat in sight, Hitler ordered the dining car destroyed so that it would not bear witness to another French triumph. After the war, a replica of the original car was built and is displayed in the Armistice

A souvenir card from the dining car where the Armistice was signed on November 11, 1918. Courtesy of the Bridgeman Art Library

Museum at the restored memorial site, now called the Glade of the Armistice in Compiegne Forest.

The tragedy that was World War I is difficult to express. But simply in terms of the railroads, it damaged rolling stock and rail lines, interrupted freight and passenger service, and disrupted food supplies throughout Europe.

In America, the impact was minor. Inconveniences like saving kitchen grease for munitions and observing meatless or wheatless days were easy adjustments to make, especially in comparison with the deprivations in Europe. Making it even less difficult, poultry was allowed on meatless days, to judge from a "Meatless Tuesday" breakfast menu of the Chicago, Milwaukee & St. Paul Railway. Along with fresh fruits and juices, hot and cold cereals, oysters cooked in various ways, grilled whitefish, broiled mackerel, and crabmeat au gratin, the menu listed half a grilled spring chicken, shredded chicken on toast, and broiled squab.[1] This hardly qualified as a sacrifice.

Soon after the war's end, the railroads recovered and roared into the 1920s. During the interwar years, rail lines proliferated and travel resumed. The railroads advertised with stunning posters showing the beauties of their destinations, from the Adirondack Mountains and Lake Placid in the Eastern United States to Rainier National Park and the Cascade Mountains in the West. English posters showed idyllic boating in Cambridge. Italian ones showed the tranquil beauty of Lake Como or Venice. French posters illustrated ancient cathedrals. The Indian State Railways depicted the majestic mountains of Kashmir. It was time to see the world—by rail.

Railroad companies competed with each other to provide more creature comforts and exclusive benefits. In America, luxury rail liners carried passengers along the East Coast to Florida's new resort communities and the sumptuous St. Augustine hotel built by Standard Oil's Henry Flagler. Elegant rail carriages and fine dining were not the only amenities in this new era as the railroads vied to offer new and distinctive features. The *Florida Special* featured a string quartet and swimsuit modeling. Women who wanted to see the latest in bathing suits probably enjoyed the fashion show, but no doubt it also appealed to male passengers.[2] In the South, the *Sunset Limited* ran between New Orleans and San Francisco in grand style. Its dining car, the *Epicure*, served "viands peculiar to the land and climate traversed."[3] The *Sunshine Special*, which ran between St. Louis and Mexico City, featured a classic American soda fountain.[4] The Great Northern Railway's luxury train was called the *Oriental Limited*, because its endpoint in Seattle was where Great Northern ships left for the ports of the Far East. In addition to fine dining, a library, buffet, and an observation car with large plate-glass windows, the *Oriental Limited* was known for its afternoon tea service. Promptly at four o'clock, a dining car waiter served tea and a uniformed maid served platters of dainty cakes to passengers. In a photograph from the era, four fashionably dressed ladies are enjoying tea together in the observation car.

The Canadian Pacific took passengers from Montreal, Quebec, in the East to Port Moody, British Colombia, in the West in luxury. However, it also offered lesser accommodations at cheap fares in an attempt to encourage the settlement of the West.[5]

In Europe, luxury rail travel returned with speed and even more panache. In 1920, one of the world's most famous trains, France's glamorous *Le Train Bleu* (the Blue Train), officially called the *Calais-Méditerranée Express*, resumed its service. Before World War I, most tourists took the train to the south of France only in winter, often traveling for their health. Wealthy British travelers in particular took *Le Train Bleu* to escape the chill of the season in England and revive themselves in the warmth of the sunny Riviera. Belgians, Russians, and eventually Americans soon followed. During the 1920s, it became fashionable to go the Riviera in the summer as well.

Le Train Bleu, so-called for its sophisticated dark blue sleeping cars, was the deluxe way to travel from Calais or Paris to Cannes, Nice, Monte Carlo, and Menton at any time of year. Its passengers included the Prince of Wales (later King Edward VIII), Charlie Chaplin, Coco Chanel,

Winston Churchill, F. Scott and Zelda Fitzgerald, and other members of the smart set. *Le Train Bleu* was modern and chic. Agatha Christie called it the millionaires' train and used it as a setting for her 1928 novel *The Mystery of the Blue Train*.

A ballet paid homage to the train. *Le Train Bleu* was a highlight of the Ballets Russes repertoire in the 1920s. One writer at the time said that it was "as difficult to get a seat for 'The Blue Train' as it is to get a seat for the thing itself during the height of the Riviera season." A virtual *Who's Who* of the era's arts was involved in its creation. Bronislava Nijinska was the choreographer, Jean Cocteau wrote the libretto, Coco Chanel designed the costumes, Anton Dolin danced the lead, and Pablo Picasso designed the curtain. The ballet was not actually set on the train. Rather it used the train's name to pay homage to the era's fashions. Impresario Serge Diaghilev said in a program note, "This being the age of speed, it already has reached its destination and disembarked its passengers."[6]

In the 1920s, a stylish London restaurant called the Blue Train featured murals by Geoffrey Houghton Brown in honor of the train. The restaurant is no more; and the murals that were painted directly on its walls have disappeared.

A more recent tribute to the train is Le Train Bleu, a restaurant hidden away at the top of Bloomingdale's department store in New York City. Unlike the exuberant Belle Époque style of the restaurant of the same name in the Gare de Lyon in Paris, Bloomingdale's Train Bleu is decorated in the more restrained Art Deco style. Modeled after the original train's dining car, its décor features mahogany paneling, mirrors, vintage lamps, brass luggage racks, plush green velvet seats, and classic white tablecloth service. Created in 1979, the restaurant was the brainchild of the late president of Bloomingdale's, Marvin Straub. The restaurant serves brunch and lunch with menu items such as steak frites, French toast made with brioche, Belgian waffles, Petrossian smoked salmon, and French pastries. It is popular with shoppers and, of course, train buffs.

Orient Express

The early years of the twentieth century, before World War I, were the glory days of the *Orient Express*. It was the train of choice for the royal and regal, where they were treated with the deference they felt they deserved and surrounded by the luxury to which they were accustomed. After the war, when the fashionable had left it for the newer *Simplon Orient Express*, the *Orient Express* still had its admirers. As late as 1935, a *Time* magazine writer described the train in classic *Time* style:

Railway glamor such as even the *20th Century Limited* never knew has ridden for half a century, still rides the *Orient Express*. For every tycoon deposited in Chicago and for every cinemactress brought to Broadway by the New York Central's famed train, the *Orient Express* has carried its kings, its Kreugers, its peacock Balkan general and as many spies as frontier guards can be bribed to pass between Europe proper and Asia improper on the musty, rattle-banging train de luxe.[7]

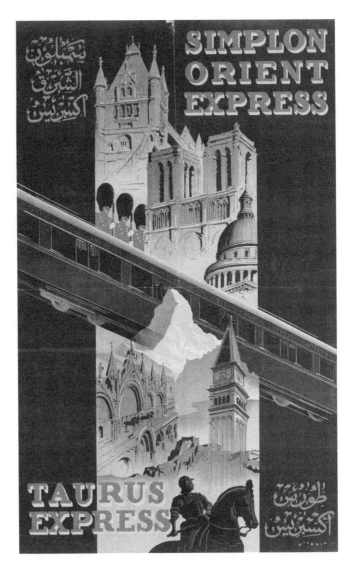

During the interwar years the *Simplon Orient Express* became the fashionable way to travel. Courtesy of the Bridgeman Art Library

In 1921, after World War I had ended and the Simplon tunnel expansion through the Alps was completed, the *Simplon Orient Express* made its debut, and chic travelers made it their train of choice. From 1919 to 1939, the deluxe *Simplon Orient Express* ran from Paris to Lausanne through the Alps to Milan and then made its way through Venice, Belgrade, and Sofia to Istanbul. It was a faster route than that of the original *Orient Express* and became the more fashionable one. According to *Time* magazine, it spanned the 1,886 miles between Paris and Istanbul in two and a half days "including all stops and fooling around at eight frontiers." Among its many amenities was a bath car with showers for passengers.[8] The *Simplon Orient Express* was the train on which Hercule Poirot was traveling when the train became snowbound, and he was confronted with the murder on the *Orient Express*.

As Agatha Christie described in *Murder on the Orient Express*, trains did become snowbound. In 1886, a train traveling from Newcastle, England to Edinburgh, Scotland, a trip that now takes less than three hours, was snowbound from Monday morning until Saturday night. The passengers had nothing to eat or drink, except melted snow, for days. Finally, crew members made it into a nearby town and "swept the town bare," according to author Sir William Acworth's account. They came back with "several hams, and roasts of beef, and shoulders of mutton, two or three clothes-baskets full of bread, and lots of tobacco."[9]

Christie's book, published in 1934, may have been more directly inspired by a snowstorm of January 1929. The *Venice Simplon Orient-Express* was on its way to Istanbul when it encountered a terrible snowstorm near Budapest. The train continued despite the weather, but just beyond the Turkish border, it became snowbound. Outside, the blizzard raged, temperatures were below zero, and all communications went down. Inside the train, there was little heat, and since the train was snowbound for nine days, the food supply was soon depleted. The only thing left was some tea. According to one passenger's report, a restaurant in a nearby village was able to supply the passengers with one meal a day, and some local peasants walked to the train and sold the stranded passengers some bread. Finally, a snow plow got through, and the train made its way to Istanbul.[10]

On another occasion, in 1931, Christie herself was stranded on the *Simplon Orient Express* when wet weather washed away part of the track. It is likely that these occurrences provided the spark for *Murder on the Orient Express*, one of her most enduring novels. Christie makes no mention of food running out on her fictional train. Happily, there was no report of murder aboard any of the actual snowbound trains.

Generally speaking, trains sped along their way without incident, and the food was more than plentiful. Passengers found it exhilarating to dine well while watching the countryside speed by. In fact, often they seemed more enthusiastic about the fact of eating aboard a train than about what they were eating. Watching the scenery sail by as you sat in the observation car, having the steward remember whether you liked to have breakfast in the dining car or in your compartment, making your menu choices as you relaxed and sipped your favorite cocktail—all these experiences were just as significant as the quality of the consommé, excellent as that may have been.

The prolific British author Beverley Nichols wrote:

> Not only does the prospect of the food allure us, but the fact that we shall be devouring it in a fantastic chariot of steel and glass, hurtling through a foreign country. There must be something seriously wrong with the man who does not enjoy lunching on a train.

Nichols wrote about his travels from Austria to Hungary and on to Greece, Turkey, and the former Palestine in the early 1930s in his *No Place Like Home*. He was enthusiastic about his lunch aboard the *Orient Express* in Hungary. It consisted of "crisp rolls, and potato mayonnaise, and veal and *petits pois* and slabs of *fromage du pays*, washed down by white wine, drunk from a tumbler (which is the only way to drink white wine)." But he was even more enthusiastic about the fact that he was eating such a lunch on a train where, he wrote, "we are alone and free, *free*. Nobody can telephone to us. . . . This is life!"[11]

Oddly, despite the many books and articles that had already proved him wrong, Nichols believed that railroads were too little praised. He wrote that although many people had "sung the romance of travelling in stage coaches, or on foot, or in small wet ships, it never seems to have occurred to anybody to sing the romance of travelling by *wagon-lit*."[12] Clearly, many others did sing the praises of trains, particularly name trains like the *20th Century*.

20th Century Limited

Certain trains capture the imagination, inspire artists, and linger in passengers' memories long after they've made their last run. The *Orient Express* was one, *Le Train Bleu* was another and, in the United States, the *20th Century Limited* was still another. New York Central's luxury train, the aptly named *20th Century* made its debut in 1902 and ran between New York and Chicago. It was faster and more expensive than other trains and was known for its exceptional service and amenities. Male passengers on the train received a boutonniere when they boarded; women were given a corsage. By its tenth anniversary, it was advertised as "The Most Famous Train in the World." When it made its last run in 1967, *The New York Times* reported it had been "known to railroad buffs for 65 years as the world's greatest train."[13] The *20th Century* inspired films and books, a play, and a Broadway musical. There was even a cocktail named after the train.

The New York Central's general passenger agent, George H. Daniels, who named the train, had also initiated the idea of Red Cap service. He introduced it in an 1896 ad that read, "Free attendant Service at Grand Central Station, N.Y. Ask the man with the RED CAP to carry your bag and show you to your cab, car, or elevated train." Other railroad companies soon copied the service.[14]

The *Century* was known for fine dining. Its earliest menus were extensive and particularly noted for offering canapés with Russian caviar. In the 1920s, its signature dishes included lake trout, broiled sweetbreads, and chicken potpie. A steward, a chef, three cooks, and seven waiters staffed its thirty-six-seat dining car.[15] It is not surprising then that like most dining car services, it was not profitable.

As excellent as it was ordinarily, the *Century* surpassed itself when it came to special occasions or special passengers. Beebe described an evening when famed opera star Nellie Melba, tenor John McCormack, violin virtuoso Fritz Kreisler, and a few others were on their way to Chicago on the *Century*. According to Beebe, the steward told the group that the chef was preparing a special dinner for them. The group enjoyed cocktails and conversation in the drawing room while they waited. Before long, the steward returned with waiters who served them a dinner consisting of hot hors d'oeuvres, crayfish court-bouillon, English Channel sole in wine and herbs, chateaubriand, and a crisp salad. Proper wines accompanied the dishes. The dessert was, naturally, Pêche Melba. According to Beebe, there was a note on the silver tray bearing the dessert. It read: "COMPLIMENTS OF THE TWENTIETH CENTURY LIMITED."[16]

The train's passenger list was often as celebrated as that of *Le Train Bleu*. In the early years, Theodore Roosevelt, William Jennings Bryan, Lillian Russell, "Diamond Jim" Brady, J.P. Morgan, and Enrico Caruso all rode the train. Later, Hollywood stars including James Cagney, Bing Crosby, and Kim Novak were among its notable passengers.

The train was renowned in the early years, but it reached its zenith when, in 1938, the new *20th Century Limited* made its debut. The new train's streamlined design epitomized the sleek sophistication of the 1930s and it became one of the most photographed symbols of the time. It was designed by the famed Henry Dreyfus, who brought his refined style to an array of other objects including the Big Ben alarm clock, the Bell telephone, and the Skyliner fountain pen, in the course of his career.

Before passengers actually boarded the *20th Century Limited*, they received the red carpet treatment—literally. At Grand Central Station, a long red carpet bearing the train's Dreyfus-designed logo was rolled out for its passengers to walk on to board the train. Although the tradition of walking on a red carpet for ceremonial purposes is, as the *Oxford English Dictionary* points out, "of great antiquity," the expression *red carpet treatment* was probably popularized by the *20th Century Limited*.

The train's interior was all sleek curved lines of gleaming aluminum and chrome. The comfortable leather seats were clustered as they might have been in a club, rather than lined up as they were on most trains. On the walls of the lounge were black and white photomurals of New York and Chicago skylines. At night, the dining car lights dimmed, and the car was transformed into the chic Café Century with music and dancing. Everything from the matchbooks to the menu covers received the Dreyfus touch.[17]

A 1938 New York Central Railroad brochure boasted that the *20th Century* provided innovations including a telephone system that "facilitates dining car reservations or the ordering of food from room service." There were "concealed radio amplifiers in the observation and dining cars" that would let passengers know about the latest world events. "A record-changing phonograph" provided after-dinner music when the dining car "magically metamorphosed into a night club." Barbers, valets, and maids were on call, and a secretary was available to help businesspeople prepare for upcoming meetings or speeches.[18]

The *Century*'s dinner menus in the 1930s were also stylishly streamlined. Typical appetizers included crab Louis cocktail, Russian caviar, and consommé. Main course choices included planked salmon steak, roast prime ribs of beef, and "Smothered veal cutlet with Mushrooms, Noodles and Prunes." For dessert, one could choose from "Green Apple Pie," "Banana Shortcake with Whipped Cream," and "N.Y.C. Baked Apple," or have a cheese course. All this plus coffee, tea, or milk cost $1.75. Passengers who wanted to splurge could opt for "Fresh Devilled Lobster, 20th Century" or "Prime Filet Mignon, Shallots Butter" for $2.35. The dining car also featured "Musical Selections by Victor Record Artists, Courtesy of R.C.A. Victor," according to the menu.

From red carpet to Red Caps, travel on the *20th Century Limited* meant being cosseted.

The Streamlined Look

During the interwar years, trains, buildings, fashions, and even men and women took on a more slender, streamlined silhouette. It was no longer fashionable to be as voluptuous as Lillian Russell. Portly men no longer looked prosperous; they looked fat. Now people wanted to look, and live, like the svelte and sophisticated "Thin Man" characters Nick and Nora Charles, played by William Powell and Myrna Loy. Menus on the streamlined trains reflected the new style. Once fashionable foods were considered old-fashioned, and newer ones took their place. Menus offered fewer courses, more à la carte options, and often fixed-price specials. One could have a meal, a snack, or a sandwich; eat in the dining car, a buffet car, or a compartment. English trains offered cocktail bars; in the United States Prohibition reigned until 1933.

Great Britain was successfully upgrading existing trains and creating new ones in the 1930s, according to author Chris de Winter Hebron, with companies competing to provide more luxurious services. Fine dining was important to these name trains. According to a contemporary report: "The serving of meals in comfort while the train is travelling at high speed is now a commonplace in railway travel. The extent to which this service is appreciated by the public can be gauged by the fact that nearly eight million meals are provided annually on British railways."[19] Upscale dining cars on trains like Great Britain's *Irish Mail* still served meals that were more elaborate than most of their counterparts, but even they had slimmer menus. The following, from 1937, was typical:

Grape Fruit
or
Cream of Lentils

Supreme of Halibut Duglèré
Roast Lamb, Mint Sauce
Baked & New Potatoes
Green Peas
or
Assorted Cold Meats
Salad

Apple Parisienne
or
Vanilla Ice
Cheese, Biscuits, Salad
Coffee[20]

Half a grapefruit, sometimes served with a maraschino cherry in its center, had become a popular starter. The fish was prepared à la Duglèré—cooked atop a bed of tomatoes, onion, shallots, thyme, bay leaf, butter, and white wine. The word *supreme*, when used with fish, means a fine fillet. Adolf Duglèré was a nineteenth-century French chef who presided over the famed Café Anglais in Paris. In addition to the fish preparation that bears his name, he was renowned for creating Pommes Anna, which consists of thinly sliced potatoes, buttered, layered in a pan, and baked. When the potatoes are done, the pan is inverted and a perfect golden brown potato cake is turned out. Even if the cake breaks when it is turned out, the dish is delectable. Duglèré was known as "the Mozart of cuisine."[21] Although it still included both a fish and a meat course, the *Irish Mail* menu was nowhere near as long and involved as menus a generation before.

By the 1930s, turtle and even mock turtle soups were seldom seen on menus. Consommé still had a place, but more often *soup of the day* was listed. Clam chowder was popular as were creamed vegetable soups. Sometimes tomato or other juices were offered as an alternative to soup. Oysters still appeared on menus, but in fewer styles. Often a menu simply listed oysters in the shell, rather than the dozen or so types previously on offer. Shrimp cocktail was served more frequently.

Generally, instead of both a fish and a meat course, diners could choose one or the other. Meats such as venison, pheasant, capon, and prairie chicken, typical choices on earlier menus, gave way to chicken, roast beef, steak, and hamburgers. Lamb won out over mutton. The enormous variety of ducks was down to, simply, duck. Fried eels, kippered herring, pickled or braised tongue, stewed tripe, and sweetbreads *en croustade* all disappeared from view. Spaghetti began to appear more frequently as Americans tentatively began their love affair with Italian food.

Potato, lobster, or chicken mayonnaise became potato, lobster, or chicken salad. Several lines featured newly popular individual salad bowls. The *20th Century*'s version was celebrated. It consisted of lettuce, finely sliced onions, radishes, cucumbers, and celery along with crumbled Roquefort cheese. Just before it was served, the cook arranged slices of tomato around it and then, at the last minute, sprinkled dressing over it. It's a simple salad, but for years passengers extolled its virtues. Ry-Krisp crackers replaced Bent's as the crackers commonly served with salads.

A few lines still offered cheese as well as dessert, but a cheese course was not as widespread as it had been. In America, English plum pudding all but disappeared as a dessert option. Naturally, the English still featured a variety of puddings.

Ice cream was popular, especially as refrigerators with freezers became available. In the United States, Jell-O, often spelled jello on menus, began popping up on dessert listings. It was wildly popular in the 1930s, as a result of its memorable jingle and the humorous ways comedian Jack Benny promoted it. He began his radio show with the greeting "Jello-O again," and often mentioned Jell-O in his skits.

In addition to lighter foods, more casual dining options, and à la carte menus, on many lines passengers could opt for fixed price special meals. They were a less expensive choice, but they had the advantage of being simpler. A typical special is this one from a 1931 Pennsylvania Railroad menu. The cost was just twenty-five cents more than a meal on the same railroad in 1899. Granted, it offered fewer courses, but a mere twenty-five cent increase in thirty years is remarkable.

Special Dinner $1.25
Please Write on Meal Check "Special Dinner"
And Each Item Desired

Veal Broth with Barley   Consomme with Vegetables
CHOICE OF:
Entrees:
Broiled Kingfish, Lemon Butter
Omelet with Creamed Shrimps
Roast Fresh Ham, Glazed Apple
Deviled Slice of Roast Beef, Mustard Sauce
Choice of Two Vegetables
Rolls or Muffins
Tea, Coffee, Cocoa or Milk

The Golden State

In California, railroads used menus, travel posters, and other publications to sell the attributes of the West Coast and its produce, from apples to oranges. A Western Pacific breakfast menu said the Golden State, California's "romantic name since the gold rush days of '49, has an extremely vital modern meaning because of the delicious gold-colored citrus fruits—principally oranges, lemons and grapefruit—which it produces in lavish abundance." The menu cover featured an illustration of an abundance of oranges along with a Franciscan Father and one of the early Missions where the men cultivated orange trees.

Grapes and raisins also were important to the California economy; however, a Western Pacific Feather River Route promotion may have been overly enthusiastic when it created a menu featuring raisins in every course. The menu celebrated California Raisin Day, April 30. It is undated, but is probably from the early years of the twentieth century. The menu recalled that in Biblical times, the children of Israel knew they had reached the Promised Land when they found grapes in the wilderness. It called California "the modern Promised Land, with smiling vineyards laden with the grapes that the children of Israel loved so well." The message closed by suggesting that one should eat raisins "every day, at every meal." This special menu honored the fruit:

Boiled Salmon Steak, California Raisin Butter
50 cents
Boiled Ham, California Raisin Sauce
50 cents
Omelet with California Raisins
45 cents
California Raisin Fritters Sabayon
25 cents
Rice Custard Pudding with California Raisins
15 cents
California Raisin Pie
10 cents
Neapolitan Ice Cream, California Raisin Cake
25 cents
California Raisin Bread
10 cents
California Raisin Gems
10 cents[22]

Another menu from the Western Pacific extolled the virtues of lettuce, another important crop in the region. The menu pointed out that California was the major source of iceberg lettuce, and suggested that it was a "gift from sun and sea." Lettuce not only offered health and appetizing values, according to the menu, but "a half a head of lettuce at the evening repast will insure a restful night." Every entrée on the menu came with a bowl of iceberg lettuce salad.

Lettuce had been a highly perishable local, seasonal vegetable; but the development of more durable lettuces, such as iceberg, allowed the new varieties to be transported without damage. As a result, lettuce production tripled during the 1920s and 1930s. Farmers in Arizona and California shipped their lettuces by train across the country. No longer seasonal or local, lettuce became a year-round product. Salads, such as the *20th Century Limited*'s, found a more prominent place on menus whether on trains, in restaurants, or in homes.[23]

Prohibition

During Prohibition, dining car drink menus featured "Cereal Beverages." Beer companies had turned to producing these so-called near beers when

When Prohibition limited U.S. train passengers to near-beer and soft drinks, waiters on English lines like the London & North Eastern Railway happily served cocktails and crusted port. Copyright © National Railway Museum/Science & Society Picture Library

they were prohibited from making the real thing. The brewers removed most of the alcohol from beer to make a drink that conformed to the law. In addition to the generic designation, cereal beverage, the near beers had names like Graino, Barlo, Bravo, Cero, Gozo, Lux-O, and Mulo. The Anheuser-Busch Company called its near beer Bevo.

Although production of cereal beverages reached over 300,000,000 gallons a year in the early 1920s, beer aficionados did not love the taste. The food writer Waverly Root said it was "such a wishy-washy, thin, ill-tasting, discouraging sort of slop that it might have been dreamed up by a Puritan Machiavelli with the intent of disgusting drinkers with genuine beer forever."[24]

The menus also offered several different brands of water including Celestine French Vichy Water, Apollinaris, Shasta, Poland Springs, and White Rock. Passengers who didn't want water or near beer could choose a Loganberry Juice High Ball or a Grape Juice High Ball as well as lemonade, fruit juices, and a variety of soft drinks.

It is difficult to imagine a restaurant menu today listing laxatives or antacids on drink menus, but it was common in the early years of the twentieth century. Pluto water, a laxative, and Bromo Seltzer, an antacid, were commonly found on the menus in the 1920s and 1930s.

Another dining car menu oddity was yeast, sold by the single cake. In *Revolution at the Table*, historian Harvey Levenstein explained that, during the 1920s, yeast sales dropped as a result of the decline of home bread baking. In response, Fleischmann's Yeast began running ads that made outlandish health food claims. Yeast, the company claimed, protected us from "two constant dangers—not having our body tissues built up and not ridding the body of poisonous waste matter." It also "prevented tooth decay, kept the intestinal canal healthy, and cured 'fallen stomach.'" As a result, Americans began spreading yeast on bread or crackers and stirring it into a glass of water, milk, or fruit juice. The Wabash passenger train *Banner Blue Limited* put it on the menu along with the waters and soft drinks. In 1938, the Federal Trade Commission ordered Fleischmann's to cease making such claims. Presumably most people went back to spreading their bread with butter. [25] It is not known whether there was a subsequent increase in fallen stomachs.

Dining car menus also listed cigars, cigarettes, chewing gum, aspirins, and playing cards. Some menus pointed out that passengers could not buy cigarettes when the train was in Iowa, Utah, or Nevada.

Passengers must have found it difficult to go without their cocktails or claret or to settle for Bevo or a grape juice highball. The railroads apparently had some problems enforcing the rules, to judge by the following message on a 1930 New Haven Railroad menu. The same message appeared on other menus during the Prohibition era as well.

> In order to avoid embarrassing situations, the management requests the co-operation of passengers in a strict observance of the Prohibition Law and requests that passengers kindly refrain from the use of intoxicating liquors as beverages while upon trains.[26]

Most writers were discreet about Prohibition law-breaking, but the ever-candid Beebe reported that Walter Chrysler Sr. founder of the car company, did not strictly observe the rules. When Chrysler traveled on the *20th Century*, according to Beebe, he always ordered fresh grapefruits to be brought to his private compartment for himself and his companions at night. After scooping out the fruit, Chrysler filled each grapefruit shell with about a half pint of cognac and set it aflame. He said that the drink that resulted was an ideal nightcap.[27]

Repeal

When Prohibition was repealed in 1933, drinks went back on the menu, and some lines created elaborately themed bar cars. Western décor was particularly popular.

The *City of Denver*, a new passenger train on the Union Pacific Railroad, made its debut on June 15, 1936, and twenty thousand people went to Denver's Union Station to see it, according to the *Denver Post*. The train's bar car was called the "Frontier Shack." The newspaper described it as a replica of the "pioneer taverns in Colorado mining towns."[28] The barkeep wore satin sleeve garters, and the knotty pine walls were covered with Wanted posters, pictures of Lillian Russell, and images of prizefighters.

Another streamliner passenger train, the *City of Los Angeles*, debuted in 1937. It ran between Chicago and Los Angeles, and was the choice of such Hollywood celebrities of the era as George Burns, Gracie Allen, and Cecil B. de Mille. The club lounge for first-class passengers was called the "Little Nugget" and was designed to look like a fantasy version of a Gold Rush era dance hall saloon. The lavish Victorian furnishings were replete with red velvet, lace, and gilded plaster cherubs.[29]

The drinks served at these whimsical bars included cocktails such as Manhattans, Martinis, Old Fashioneds, Gin Fizzes, and Benedictine & Brandy. One could order imported Scotch, rye whiskey, bourbon, cognac, gin, and a variety of beers and ales. A few of the mineral waters of the Prohibition years were still sold, as were some soft drinks.

Vodka is conspicuous by its absence. Today the United States is the second-largest consumer of vodka in the world, after Russia. But until the 1960s, Americans didn't drink much vodka. Rudolph Kunett, a Russian émigré who was part of the Smirnoff family, began distilling and selling vodka in the United States shortly after Repeal. However, the new to Americans liquor didn't sell well until it was advertised as "Smirnoff White Whisky— No Smell, No Taste." The slogan hinted that you could drink it and go back to the office or home without the telltale breath you would have if you drank whiskey or gin. But the Cold War and anti-Soviet sentiment depressed sales, which had not been strong enough to stand up to the challenge.[30]

Then, in 1962, James Bond stepped up to the bar. When Sean Connery, star of the film "Dr. No," ordered a martini made with Smirnoff vodka and, famously, asked that it be shaken, not stirred, vodka sales took off. Interestingly, in the first of Ian Fleming's James Bond books, *Casino Royale*, the martini he called the Vesper was made with Gordon's gin, vodka, and Kina Lillet.[31]

However, according to Patricia Herlihy, author of *Vodka: A Global History*, Americans should thank Richard Nixon for making vodka so popular. He arranged a business deal between Pepsi-Cola and Stolichnaya vodka, and sent vodka sales soaring. Stoli became the *in* drink and in 1975, vodka became the country's leading liquor.[32]

Children Onboard

The sophisticated adult traveler was not the only dining car customer. By the 1920s, many railroads—along with hotels and restaurants—had instituted children's menus. From the railroad's point of view, children's menus were a good way to cultivate the next generation of customers. Now commonplace, children's menus were an innovation at the time. Previously, many parents had packed food for the children rather than take them to the dining car. Some trains had allowed parents to simply share their meals with their child. Some had offered half portions of adult meals at half price for children under ten or twelve.

Parents appreciated the fact that the railroads charged less for the special children's meals than their adult counterparts. Portions were child-size, and the foods were bland in keeping with nutritional theories of the early twentieth century. A children's menu from the Canadian National Railways noted that the items were selected after consultation with a well-known dietitian and were suitable for children up to ten years of age. It also noted, "In addition to the menu proper, there are pictures printed in blue and brown and verses that appeal to children's fancy."[33]

Railroads began offering meals and menus designed especially for children in the 1920s. This one is from the St. Louis–San Francisco Railway Company. Courtesy of the Special Collections and Archives Missouri State University

The menus themselves were designed to appeal to children. Some were in the shape of animals like squirrels or elephants. Some featured Mother Goose rhymes, especially food-centered ones like "Jack Sprat" who could eat no fat or "Little Tommy Tucker" who had to sing for his supper. Some menus were puzzles; others featured illustrations kids could color. The menus also gave meals names intended to amuse children, such as the Box Car Lunch or the Coal Car Special.

Often, children's menus were educational. A Union Pacific Railroad menu from the forties featured drawings of Kaibab squirrels and information about their habits along with menu choices. When children read the menu, or when mom or dad read it to them, they could learn that the squirrel lived only on the north rim of the Grand Canyon. As they decided on their dessert, they would find out that he had a white tail, which he used to hide his dark coat when it snowed.

A typical menu offered vegetable soup or chicken broth, a broiled lamb chop, mashed potatoes, a fresh vegetable, bread and butter and a choice of

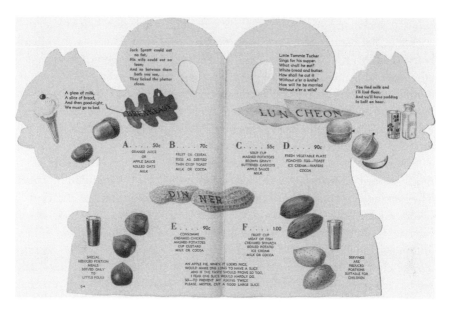

Nursery rhymes made children's menus fun to read. Courtesy of the Special Collections and Archives Missouri State University

desserts including ice cream, cup custard, fruit, or jam. The price of fifty-five cents also included either milk or cocoa.

An undated St. Louis–San Francisco Railway menu listed choices for children including a meal consisting of consommé, creamed chicken, mashed potatoes, cup custard, milk or cocoa for ninety cents. Another option included fruit cup, meat or fish, creamed spinach, boiled potato, ice cream, milk, or cocoa for a dollar. Still another, less expensive menu featured a soup cup, mashed potatoes, brown gravy, buttered carrots, apple sauce, and milk for fifty cents. There were also à la carte choices including cereal, juices, and toast.

A ten-year-old child who traveled in style in the early 1930s might have developed a fondness for luxury railroads, but by the time he or she was twenty the world had changed. When the children of the early 1930s reached adulthood, they faced war, food rationing, and a world that valued automobiles and airplanes above railroads.

Soda Fountains

The Temperance movement and Prohibition were a boon to the soda fountain business. The soda fountain replaced the barroom in towns across the country, and many drinkers settled for sodas and sundaes in lieu of beer and cocktails. Per capita ice cream consumption leapt from less than five quarts before 1920 to nine quarts by 1930. With improved refrigeration and more efficient ice cream making equipment, it was easier than ever to install a soda fountain, and they were installed nearly everywhere, in corner drugstores, department stores, on luxury ocean liners, and on trains. In 1926, the Northern Pacific Railroad equipped ten of its new Pullman observation cars with soda fountains. Others followed its example.

Sundaes were among America's favorite soda fountain treats, and an enormous amount of creativity went into making and, especially, naming them. They included—but were not limited to—the Bachelor Sundae, the Boston Club Sundae, the Delmonico, Merry Widow, Hawaiian Special, Easter Sundae, Coney Island, Aviation Glide, Throwover, Knickerbocker Glory, and more. One of the more whimsical was the Chop Suey Sundae. Recipes for the chop suey sauce varied enormously. Except for the "lychu-nuts" this recipe called for, the sauces had nothing to do with the Chinese-American restaurant dish of the same name.

ᐁ Dry Chop Suey Sundae

Chop and mix ½ pound seeded raisins, ¼ pound lychu-nuts, ⅛ pound cocoanut, ½ pound candied cherries, ½ pound candied pineapple, ½ pound of mixed nuts, ⅛ pound citron and ½ pound of dates. To serve place the ice cream in the sundae glass and sprinkle with the mixture, and add a little powdered cinnamon.

—Irving P. Fox, *The Spatula, An Illustrated Monthly Publication for Druggists,* 1906

California's Bounty

Railroad companies often stressed that many of the foods served in their dining cars were fresh from the regions the trains traveled. The Southern Pacific, in particular, emphasized "Western products for western consumption" in its dining cars. In the 1920s, Southern Pacific publications reported that its dining cars served the finest, freshest local cantaloupes, apples, grapes, oranges, raisins, and other produce. A tomato variety grown in the Sacramento, California, area was publicized as a "Sacratomato."

Dining car menus featured California ripe olives, California fruits, even California cream cheese. Raisins were an important crop and in a 1904 booklet titled "Eat California Fruit," extolling their virtues, it was suggested that since raisins are "a natural confection" they should be given to children in lieu of candy. Recipes for raisin cookies, cakes, breads, stuffing for turkey, and puddings were included in the booklet.

This contemporary recipe for Raisin Grower's Raisin Sauce is a traditional accompaniment to ham, but would be equally welcome with chicken or turkey.

⌒ Raisin Grower's Raisin Sauce

Yields: 2 cups

    1 cup firmly packed brown sugar
    1½ tablespoons cornstarch
    ¼ teaspoon ground cinnamon
    ¼ teaspoon ground cloves
    ¼ teaspoon dry mustard
    ¼ teaspoon salt
    1¾ cups water
    1 cup California raisins
    1 tablespoon vinegar

In a saucepan, combine brown sugar, cornstarch, spices, mustard, and salt. Stir in water and raisins. Cook over moderate heat, stirring constantly, until mixture thickens and boils. Remove from heat; blend in vinegar. Serve warm with ham.

—Courtesy of the California Raisin Marketing Board

CHAPTER 6

❦

The Golden—and
Not So Golden—Era

From a long-distance railroad passenger's point of view, the interwar years were golden. Trains took travelers to their destinations faster and in more luxury than ever. Railways added perquisites and benefits that made rail travel better than ever. In England, cinema cars showed newsreels, cartoons, and travelogues. U.S. trains employed nurse/stewardesses to help mothers with babies and the elderly on their travels. Trains introduced observation cars with wide expanses of glass for scenic viewing. Dining, even in the buffets and bar cars, was delightful. Service was impeccable. There was no better or faster way to travel long distances.

More than a billion passengers traveled on U.S. railroads in 1920, and by 1925 at their peak of popularity, the dining cars employed 10,000 people.[1] Private varnish was still a status symbol for the very wealthy in the Roaring Twenties; in 1927, builders manufactured more than one hundred of the luxurious rail cars.

At the time, some people believed that the automobile would be a passing fad, despite the fact that it was already beginning to take business away from local commuter trains. But it had little or no impact on the long-distance trains, with their splendid drawing room, sleeping, and dining cars. Sensible people did not want to drive all the way across Europe or America in an unreliable automobile when they could enjoy the elegant surroundings and excellent service of a first-class railway carriage.

At the 1915 Panama-Pacific International Exposition in San Francisco, visitors had watched in amazement as aviator Allan H. Loughead (who later

The caption on this 1935 photograph read: "Sliding partitions between connecting double bedrooms permit this family to breakfast in negligee privacy." Courtesy of the Archives Center, National Museum of American History, Smithsonian Institution

changed his name to the easier to pronounce Lockheed) took brave visitors on flights in his aeroplane. As impressed as they were, it is unlikely that the fairgoers imagined themselves crossing the world, or even the country, in a plane. When Charles Lindberg flew across the Atlantic in 1927, few people—least of all railroad executives—saw the change in travel his flight portended or thought planes would soon compete with trains.

However, even if the airlines had not arrived and the good times had lasted, the railroads had a problem. In 1925, U.S. railroads served 80,000 meals a day, and endured a net loss of $10.5 million.[2] Costs were rising faster than revenues. Something had to be done. Railroad companies sought different ways to lessen their losses without losing their reputation for first-class travel. They couldn't simply cut services. Wealthy passengers were accustomed to having the railroads provide them with every luxury and did not want that to change. When a railroad tried to eliminate frills, passengers noticed and complained. Fresh flowers in dining cars were expensive; but when the Southern Pacific substituted plastic flowers, passengers let the company know they were not pleased.[3] How to cut losses while maintaining the impression, and public relations value, of first-class service was the challenge.

In the United States, Prohibition didn't help. Alcohol sales are always a good profit generator for restaurants, and dining cars were no exception. Prior to Prohibition, dining car menus featured long lists of wines, champagnes, and other drinks. In fact, the standard by which a smooth ride was judged was typically that the champagne didn't spill. During the dry years, some menus featured long lists of sweets and soft drinks to try to make up for the lack of alcohol. But losing that source of revenue in 1920 was a blow to U.S. railroad dining services just as it was to restaurants and hotels.

And then the Depression hit. By 1933, overall ridership in America had fallen from one billion in 1920 to just 435 million.[4] The market for private varnish cars collapsed, with only one built in 1930.[5]

Although the European lines did not have to cope with Prohibition, they did have the Depression. Railroad companies everywhere tried various strategies to cope with their losses. Most were unsuccessful. Several companies added some form of air conditioning to their cars in the 1930s. Some counted on faster trains to improve business. In 1933, a new German train, aptly named the *Fliegnede Hamburger* (Flying Hamburger), traveled at 100 miles an hour. Not to be outdone, one of England's streamlined locomotives hit the previously unimagined speed of 126 miles an hour just a few years later.

To cut costs, some railroads dropped dining cars. Others continued to run them and even build new ones in the hope that newer, shinier cars would bring passengers back. At the time, on average, a new dining car cost more than $50,000, not including the cost of outfitting it with china, silver, and linens. Especially luxurious cars were even more expensive. The new *20th Century* diners were $92,000 each.[6] Repairs and upkeep were also costly. A typical diner needed an overhaul every eighteen months at a cost of up to $7,000. Since dining car crew salaries were among the largest expenses, railroads increased dining options like lunch counters and buffets because they required fewer staff. Some railroad companies hired women as servers since they could be paid less than men.[7] The strategy was similar to Pullman's when he had hired freed slaves because they would work for lower salaries than whites.

In Europe, Wagon-Lit followed the example of other European and American railway companies and added second-class cars. In Great Britain, railways had second- and third-class fares and also tried various other ways to control costs while still offering dining services. Since railway competition at the time included buses that offered cheaper fares than trains but no food service, railways advertised the quality and convenience of their restaurant cars. When they finally recognized the threat posed by the nascent air travel industry, railways stressed the luxury and comfort of train travel.

Quick Meals and Snacks

As far back as 1883, Pullman had introduced buffet cars to give passengers a place to enjoy light refreshment between meals. The *Railroad Gazette* reported in December 1887 that among the many features of the New York Central's Vestibule Train was a buffet car with "an unobtrusive bar, and the proper antidotes are carried in a medicine chest in the same car."[8] Using medical vocabulary in speaking about drinks was common at the time. The preeminent bartender Jerry Thomas referred to bar patrons as "*patients*" in his 1862 book *How to Mix Drinks, or The Bon-Vivant's Companion.*[9]

In 1894, *The New York Times* reported that the buffet cars "with meals served à la carte, appear to be coming much into favor." By the interwar years, they had arrived. Railroad companies liked buffet cars because they were less expensive to equip and run than dining cars. In fact, and in contrast to most dining cars, they were generally profitable. Passengers liked the buffets because they were more casual, less expensive, and quicker than formal dining car experience.

In general, buffet cars offered lunches, snacks, and light refreshments such as oyster stews, soups, tea, coffee, and drinks. Many still offered a very good dinner, but it was less formal and expensive than those of the earlier years. Champagne stayed on the menu. The New Haven Railroad's buffet cars running between Boston and New York in the early twentieth century featured Medford (Massachusetts) rum, Krug champagne, Boston scrod, and Cotuit oysters.[10]

Boston scrod is a Northeast U.S. seafood term for filet of cod, haddock, or other whitefish. Legends about the name abound. Some say it's an acronym for Seaman's Catch Received On Deck. Others claim it's shorthand for Sacred Cod and refers to the Atlantic cod carved from pine that hangs in the Boston State House in tribute to the fish that fed the state's early settlers. The *Oxford English Dictionary* (OED) gives its etymology as possibly Middle Dutch, *schrode* meaning "piece cut off." The OED goes on to report that some U.S. dictionaries define the verb *scrod* as "to shred, to prepare for cooking by tearing in small pieces." Whatever the derivation of the word, scrod was a feature on the trains and remains a popular fish in the Northeast.

In addition to the buffet cars, other economical dining options included café cars, bar cars, lounges, café-lounge-observation cars, coffee shop cars, soda fountains, and lunch counter cars. The same train might offer a dining car, a café car, and a lunch counter car so that passengers could choose whichever they preferred.

In England, buffet cars were introduced on some lines in the late 1800s, but initially they were not well received. They were soon converted back to regular dining cars. Some thought their lack of success was due to the fact that they looked like working-class pubs and that the cars were open to all classes of passengers. They believed that some passengers wouldn't want to mix with members of the working class, and others would find rubbing elbows with the upper classes intimidating. Chris de Winter Hebron, author of *Dining at Speed: A Celebration of 125 Years of Railway Catering,* disagreed. He thought their lack of success was more likely because passengers had been accustomed to being served at a table, not walking up to a counter for service. However, when more elegant Pullman buffet cars were introduced in 1910, passengers happily enjoyed their snacks and gin and tonics on the new cars.

A typical 1930s English buffet car lunch offered choices including grapefruit, tomato soup, veal and ham pie, ham, pressed beef, ox tongue, galantine of chicken, roast beef, potato salad, fruit salad or cheese and biscuits, rolls and butter, and tea or coffee. With the exception of the tomato soup, everything was cold, which meant it could be prepared and ready ahead of time. Serving food cold also saved on fuel costs. English "Quick Lunch Cars," were very like American lunch counters with bar seating and service from a grill and hot plate.

In addition to buffet cars, some English lines found flexible ways to meet passengers' needs by featuring specific meals or snacks at particular times. They ran breakfast cars for businessmen on early morning runs, tea cars in the afternoon. On the tea cars, a "pantry boy" served tea sandwiches and cakes from a portable wooden stand of the type commonly used in fashionable English tearooms. Some lines featured luncheon cars geared to shoppers, and some advertised an 11:15 p.m. post-theatre train serving late-night suppers.[11]

The English also economized by trimming their dining car menus. Some lines eliminated hors d'oeuvres, starting menus with soup instead. They offered a cold fish course and one roast, with assorted cold meats as an alternative. Either a sweet or cheese was offered for dessert, but not both. In addition, they planned menus across the entire line to allow increased buying in bulk. The French railroads also instituted buffet car service to help economize, with meals served at seats on removable tables. German trains offered quick meals consisting of drinks and cold refreshments on portable tables at the passenger's seat.

The Luxury-Economy Dichotomy

Even as railroads tried to economize with buffet, café, and lunch cars, they continued to introduce new luxury cars and promote fine dining. Hebron put the dichotomy in perspective when he wrote that the fast, sophisticated streamliners were "attention-getters. These trains formed only a small proportion of the passenger services but they had tremendous publicity value—they made rail travel feel glamorous."[12]

A perfect example of an attention-getter was the New Haven Railroad's *Yankee Clipper*, an all-parlor car train that ran between Boston and New York. It made its debut in 1930, just a year after the 1929 stock market crash. Called the "Aristocrat of Trains," it offered the finest foods and service. The stewards wore tuxedos; waiters wore white suits and black bow ties. The line claimed to use only fresh foods, nothing was canned. Every afternoon, a proper British tea complete with crumpets and finger sandwiches was served. The passengers could opt to have their tea in the parlor car or the dining car.

The dining car's dinner menu was extensive, if not adventurous. Along with the inevitable oysters, consommé, and roast beef, it featured local favorites like Boston fish chowder, clam fritters, and fresh strawberry shortcake. It was very much the sort of menu one would find at a good restaurant in a New England city of the day. Everything was high-quality, but familiar. It was not French cuisine.

Just seven years later, the railroad introduced its streamlined "Self-Service Grill Cars." Obviously designed to cut costs, the grill cars were outfitted with charcoal grills and steam tables, but no ovens. Breads, pies, and cakes were baked off the train at the company's Dover Street cook car in South Boston. Roasts, turkeys, and other meats were also cooked there, to be served onboard the trains.

The foods included New England clam chowder, charcoal broiled chicken with vegetables, charcoal broiled fish (type not specified), and baked smoked ham with pineapple. Desserts included Indian pudding à la mode, vanilla ice cream, and "Our Own" apple pie. The grill car menus prominently featured cocktails, since by then Prohibition had ended.

The original intent behind the grill cars was that passengers would walk up to the counter, order their food, and then carry it back to their seats on a tray. Requiring no waiters, no oven, and fewer cooks, the streamlined service was good for the railroad. In theory, its informality and freshly grilled food would appeal to passengers. They did.

What passengers did not like was the lack of service. So many people complained about the difficulty of carrying trays full of food on a swaying train that the railroad had to hire servers. Reportedly, female passengers had the most difficulty carrying their own food. However, in response to the problem, the New Haven hired female servers. They were called "Grill Girls," and in that less-enlightened time were required to be young, slender, and attractive. They wore skirt suits, perky hats, and sensible shoes, and were prominently featured in grill car advertising.[13]

The contrast between cutting corners, on the one hand, and offering luxury service, on the other, was typical of railroads during the interwar years.

Lounge cars offered casual food service in comfortable surroundings as this circa 1940 photograph shows. Courtesy of the Archives Center, National Museum of American History, Smithsonian Institution

Off the Train

One of the most effective ways for the railroads to economize and to make food provisioning more efficient was to move some of the storage, preparation, and cooking off the train. In the earliest days of dining cars, the kitchens were tiny and menus were grand. When Mrs. Frank Leslie, wife of the publisher of *Frank Leslie's Illustrated Newspaper*, traveled on a luxury Pullman car in 1877, she described her dinner as "Delmonican" and wrote that the train's kitchen reminded her of "the little Parisian *cuisines*, where every inch of space is utilized and where such a modicum of wood and charcoal provides such marvelous results."[14]

Years later, menus were shorter and dining car kitchens were larger, but producing such results was still a challenge. Railroad passengers consumed enormous quantities of food each day. A typical train might use more than a ton of potatoes and hundreds of pounds of other vegetables and fruits, every day. A dining car chef cannot have the train stop to pick up extra eggs or cheese if supplies run out; and baking enough bread for more than 300 meals a day in a small railway kitchen is impractical, even if it is possible. So, in order to make supplying, storing, and cooking food more efficient and reliable, railroads built commissaries with fully equipped kitchens, butchering facilities, bakeries, laundries, and storage areas at strategic points along a line.

In 1914, the Northern Pacific, of Great Big Baked Potato fame, built a commissary where foods were stored and prepared in Seattle. The building was topped with a forty-foot long replica of its famous baked potato to keep it in the public eye. The company operated its own dairy, poultry, and hog farms to ensure both supply and quality. It labeled its eggs and dairy products with the date to keep track of freshness. This was in the early years of the twentieth century; long before use-by or sell-by dating was known. No wonder the Northern Pacific was known for the superiority of its food.[15]

In 1922, the *Southern Pacific Railway Bulletin* featured an article titled, "The Story Back of a Southern Pacific Menu," to explain to passengers how the railway maintained the "Highest Standard of Fare and Service" over 11,000 miles of line. The article offers insight into the problems of all railroads offering food service and the solutions they attempted to find.

Clearly the Southern Pacific took pride in its meal service. Under the heading "The Best of Everything," the article reported that the railroad bought the "finest oranges and grape-fruit from California, alligator pears [avocados] from Florida and California, Louisiana rice, Coachella Valley melons . . . Fresno grapes and raisins, Hood River apples." It also boasted that it was the only company that obtained its maple syrup from Vermont and that it was "pure maple syrup, unmixed with sugar."

At the time, the Southern Pacific served nearly 8,000 meals a day in ninety-two dining cars, one café car, and twelve lunch cars. A typical kitchen on one of its dining cars measured six feet eight inches by sixteen feet and included a range, oven, charcoal broiler, ice chest, sink, and table. According to the *Southern Pacific Railway Bulletin*, the Pacific system's daily requirements included 514 gallons of milk, 3,226 pounds of potatoes, 172 gallons of cream, 597 pounds of butter, 803 dozen eggs, 2,148 pounds of beef, 503 pounds of coffee, and 23 boxes of apples.

The cars were not yet equipped with refrigerators, so they needed between 1,000 and 2,000 pounds of ice a day. The ice was stored under the cars and was accessible only when the train was stopped. This was also a time before dishwashers and on a typical day one man would have to wash nearly 22,000 dishes. In 1926, according to another one of its pamphlets, the Southern Pacific Railway dining car department served 7,182,000 meals, "representing sufficient food to serve at one sitting the entire population of the State of Illinois."

It is little wonder that the railroads would try to move as much equipment and work as possible off the train and into commissary storerooms and kitchens. Not only did that relieve some of the pressure on the trains' kitchen crews, but it also allowed for bulk purchasing, saved money, and helped ensure consistency. Because the commissary kitchen staff did much of the work, it was easier for the train's cooks to finish the dishes the same way every time. The sauce that accompanied the steak would not differ from one day to the next. Freshly baked apple pie needed only to be loaded onboard, sliced, topped with a scoop of ice cream, and served to a delighted diner. Passengers could be sure a dish they enjoyed on one trip would look and taste just as good on the next.

The Southern Pacific operated six commissaries where kitchen equipment and foodstuffs were stored and at least partially cooked. The line even built its own smokehouse where cooks prepared hams and bacon. According to the *Southern Pacific Railway Bulletin*, in its commissary kitchens:

> All meat is boned, trimmed, cut and made ready for cooking before delivery to the chefs. Stocks are prepared for soups and issued to the cars in gallon containers. Mayonnaise and French dressings are prepared and issued in quart Mason jars. . . . Pie dough is made in the Commissary and issued to the cars to be kept in the chill boxes and matured for use. Prunes are cooked and issued in half gallon containers so that the quality can be uniform. Bread, biscuits and pies for the first meal on the road are also baked in the Commissary kitchens.

The commissaries' large storerooms allowed railroads to save by buying in quantity. Providing convenient storage space where the train could be resupplied along its route also freed up space aboard the train. Dining car supplies—from wine glasses to pots and pans to cooks' aprons—were cleaned, polished, and stored in the commissaries ready to equip a train for its run or to replace items that might have broken or worn out during a trip. The Southern Pacific trains had to be stocked with more than 2,000 pieces of linen for a three-day run. That included 1,000 napkins, 220 tablecloths, and 250 doilies as well as cooks' aprons and waiters' coats. The linens were washed, ironed, and stored at the commissary laundry, so they would be ready for the next trip. Some commissaries had humidors where they kept cigars and cigarettes fresh for passengers.

Commissaries also functioned as office space where the chef or steward in charge planned menus, ordered supplies, and balanced the books. He made sure that everything a particular dining car had listed on the day's menu was ready to load onboard the minute the train pulled up. He simplified work for the dining car crew and made sure everything ran smoothly. Training programs for cooks and waiters were also held in the commissary buildings.[16]

Most railroads in the United States and elsewhere had similar operations. In Paris, an enormous plant supplied thousands of breads, cakes and pastries, cold meats and poultry to the many Wagon-Lits trains. Foods were brought in from all corners of the country, checked, cleaned, wrapped, and sent to the terminal. The railroad also arranged for supplies of regional specialties and fresh breads, produce, and milk to be stored and ready at stops along the route.[17]

The Unseen Service

Over time, most railroads increased their reliance on off-train food preparation and began using canned, frozen, and premade foods to cut costs. In 1930, the Great Northern Railway published a pamphlet describing the behind-the-scenes workings of the commissary department employees. Aptly titled "The Unseen Service," it was distributed to passengers to show them how serious the line was about providing them with the best service, whether seen or unseen. The brochure naturally described the "Unseen Service" as completely positive and customer-oriented. It did not point out that it saved the railroad money or that it allowed them to staff the trains with fewer people or that skilled cooks might be replaced with unskilled workers who simply heated already cooked foods. The service was unseen; some of the rationale behind it went unexplained.

Baking bread for the Atchison, Topeka & Santa Fe Railroad in 1943. Courtesy of the Library of Congress

The Pennsylvania Railroad's 1938 service manual promised, "dishes that please the eye, delight the taste, satisfy the appetite." The manual insisted on high standards and reported that the cooks made all soups and sauces from scratch. It noted that, "under no circumstances shall cooked vegetables be carried from one meal to another." Conversely, it suggested that leftover vegetables could be made into "palatable salads."

The manual was scrupulous about accuracy in menu descriptions. A recipe for baked beans instructed, "If Baked Beans are represented on Menu as 'Home Style' the following recipe is to be used. If 'Home Style' is not represented, canned beans are to be used in preparation of dishes listed below."

Portions were generous. One serving of fresh fish was a full pound, raw. Exceptions were shrimp, where one portion was one-third of a pound, and scallops, one-quarter of a pound. One portion of lobster was one and a quarter pounds. Steak and hamburger portions were half pounds; pork was a generous full pound.

Service and presentation instructions were as specific as recipes. Nothing was left to chance or to the staff's discretion. Detailed instructions spelled out which plate was to go under a cocoa or coffee pot, and directed that canapés were to be served on a bread and butter plate with a branch of parsley and one-eighth of a lemon. There were directions for making radish roses, cherry poinsettias, celery curls and other decorative touches.

Clearly, the company cared about quality. It even had instructions for making caviar canapés and classic French sauces. Yet rather than more perishable and expensive fresh vegetables, the railroad served canned ones, including asparagus, green beans, beets, corn, peas, and tomatoes, and "Frosted Vegetables" such as asparagus, broccoli, spinach, and cauliflower. It used tea bags, rather than loose tea. There was a recipe for "Homemade" gingerbread and another for one made from a prepared mix.[18]

Some of its money-saving methods recall similar ones from Rufus Estes in the early 1900s. The Pennsylvania manual suggested toasting leftover bread and serving it in lieu of crackers with soup. Leftover celery was to be saved for the chef's stocks and soups. Meats could be chopped and used in hashes and stews. All of which are sensible, thrifty kitchen practices.

A few years later, a Union Pacific manual included recipes for cakes made with Betty Crocker cake mix. The New Haven Railroad's famed and acclaimed Welsh rarebit came from a jar. It was a jar from S.S. Pierce, Boston's finest grocer, but a jar nonetheless.[19] In 1941, the Wabash dining car featured an ad for "American Lady Brand" consommé on its menu and noted that it was "Sold at Good Food Stores Everywhere." Using canned foods had become so acceptable that dining car menus could advertise them. By then, most lines were taking such short cuts to economize and make food service more uniform and predictable. Certainly they had to be economical, but some of the practices used by railroads in the late 1930s were leading to lower standards.

Other Options

In the late 1930s, railroad passenger business picked up, but dining services continued to face the same challenges as ever. In addition to off-train preparations and other options, some railroads reduced portion sizes. Some offered fewer choices on à la carte menus and shorter complete meal menus. They even used fewer plates.

On its *Yellowstone Comet* dining car, the Northern Pacific offered five short set menus ranging in price from seventy-five cents to a dollar. One of the seventy-five cent menus consisted of chilled tomato bouillon, crab or chicken salad, Vienna rolls with butter, and iced tea or coffee. The dollar menu was lettuce or tomato; choice of meat or fish; Northern Pacific Big Baked Potato; choice of one vegetable; pie, pudding, or ice cream; and coffee, iced tea, or milk. The heading on the menu was a true departure. Rather than the formal title of "Dinner Menu," the heading was a casual "Evening Club Service." Less formal, less grand, more relaxed meals were the order of the day.

Preparing food off the train also allowed for special buffet services like that introduced in 1940 by the New Haven Railroad. To accommodate increasing passenger traffic, the New Haven replaced one dining car on both the eastbound and westbound *Merchants Limited* with a buffet car. The dining cars that were replaced were used on other passenger trains. The buffet cars were remodeled passenger cars outfitted with dining-car-style tables and chairs and a long buffet table, but without a kitchen. A hostess, a team of waiters, and a buffet chef wearing an impressive white uniform and a traditional chef's toque staffed the car. Two shining copper chafing dishes held the day's specials—perhaps a broiled leg of lamb with mint sauce or lobster Newburg served on toast—and kept them hot. A selection of vegetables and a potato dish completed the menu. The meal cost passengers less than a typical dining car dinner and, much to passengers' delight, second helpings were complimentary. Because the buffet car did not have a kitchen, the food served was either prepared off the train at the company's Dover Street cook car or in the remaining dining car.[20]

Chafing dishes have a long history, but they were particularly fashionable at the time. A chafing dish buffet presided over by a man dressed in chef's whites must have felt different and sophisticated to passengers. Because the buffet allowed the train to serve more passengers more quickly and to operate with fewer employees, it must have felt like good business to the New Haven's bookkeepers.

Family-style service and off-peak hour dining were other cost-cutting measures that helped both the railroad and the passengers save money. A 1940 Pennsylvania Railroad Menu offered early- or late-bird specials. To ease traffic in the dining car and the kitchen, the line offered special low-cost meals to those who were willing to eat earlier or later than the main rush. A breakfast of orange juice, minced ham with scrambled eggs, toast, and coffee was just fifty cents when served before seven. The "Special Plate" luncheon was served before eleven or after two; the dinner, before five and after eight. Lunch and dinner each cost sixty-five cents and consisted of the following simple menu:

Fish, Meat or Egg dish
(Omelet if desired)
Served on a large plate, family style
With Potatoes and Vegetable
Bread and Butter
Dessert
Cup of Coffee, Tea or Glass of Milk

Another smart business decision was to run ads on dining car menus, like the one for canned American Lady Brand Consommé. In the late 1930s and 1940s, railroad menus advertised beers, Kentucky bourbon, rye whiskey, Canada Dry ginger ale, and soda water. By twenty-first century standards, some of the ads are offensive and some are silly. But no doubt the advertising brought in needed revenues.

A 1930s Budweiser beer ad showed a black man in formal waiter's attire serving bottles of beer at what seemed to be a sophisticated cocktail party. The ad headline read, "Good Times Coming, Boss!" An ad in the same era for Pabst Blue Ribbon Beer showed a white woman in a typical maid's outfit serving at an equally posh-looking party. It was headlined, "A Sunday Supper Success." The copy read, "Animated amber and old gold, a crown of lacy foam, beautiful to behold, and all that it promises to the palate—Pabst Blue Ribbon Beer."

Other ads ran for hotels including the Waldorf Astoria, Hotel Edison, Lincoln Hotel, and the Dinkler Hotels, a southern chain. Marshall Field, the Chicago department store, ran ads on menus as did S&W Cafeterias.

World War II

In Europe, the war was devastating to railways. When France fell in 1940, the German military took control of European trains, including the *Orient Express*. By then, all pleasure travel had ended. In addition to transportation, the military used some carriages for officers' quarters; some sleeper cars were said to have been used as brothels. Dining cars became stationary restaurants or troop canteens. Hundreds of cars were sabotaged, plundered, or destroyed during the war.

When the war ended, the cars that did survive required extensive re-building, from the locomotives to the kitchens. Camouflaged cars had to be

" ..... and twenty more for
dinner just coming in ...."

British Railways have little or no surplus margin of food
for unexpected guests. They are rationed just as you are!
For the same reason, Refreshment Baskets
have had to be abolished.

Food rationing was a challenge for railroads in England during and after the war years. Copyright © National Railway Museum/ Science & Society Picture Library

repainted. Draperies and upholstered furnishings had to be replenished. In the dining cars, everything from the china to the cooking equipment needed to be replaced. Restoring Europe's railway system would be the work of years.

In the United States, the situation was entirely different. The financial problems that had plagued the railroads came to an end. The war turned out to be profitable for U.S. railroads as both freight and passenger service increased dramatically. Troop trains accounted for much, but not all, of the increase in business. Many members of the military traveled on regular passenger trains, whether on furlough or en route to report for duty. Civilians were urged to forego rail travel for the war effort; but faced with gas and tire rationing, those who had to travel took the train. To handle the surge in business, rail cars that had been sidelined because of the drop in business before the war were taken out of storage and put back to use. Eventually the government allowed the building of 1,200 new troop cars and 400 troop kitchen cars.[21]

The increase in business meant a huge increase in demands on the railroads. Many of their seasoned employees, including cooks, had gone into the military. Those who were left had to work longer and longer hours. They also had to make do with less. Foods including butter, meat, and coffee were rationed, so railroad cooks had to devise ways to feed more passengers with the changes in supplies. Some cut their coffee with fillers. Margarine appeared on tables in lieu of butter. Fish and turkey were served more often than beef.

Some dining service niceties had to go. Fine Irish linens were no longer available, so as tablecloths and napkins wore out, they were replaced with ordinary cotton ones. Rather than the elaborate place settings of the past, meals were served on one plate with a fork, knife, and spoon. Storing, serving, and washing such specialized items as salad plates, fish forks, and dessert spoons was impossible when 600 people might be served on a train that once carried 200.[22]

Service standards suffered everywhere. The Fred Harvey Company, which still owned some Harvey Houses and staffed dining cars on the Santa Fe Railroad, was faced with a huge influx of business when the railroads began transporting troops across the country. Before the war, business had been so slow that journalist William Allen White had written an obituary for the Harvey Houses, saying they had been "beacons of culinary light and learning."[23] With the wartime increase in business, suddenly the company sprang back to life. It had to reopen closed Harvey Houses, hire new waitresses, and bring others back from retirement. The company needed many employees—fast. As a result, the old rules for Harvey Girls, like promising to stay for six to nine months and not to marry, were dropped. Married, divorced, over thirty—as long as they were willing to work, they were hired. The company even hired high school girls in summer. There wasn't time for the rigorous training in the "Harvey way" new employees once received. As soon as they were hired, they went to work, and they worked long hours.

One positive, but unintended, consequence of the wartime increase in hiring was that the Harvey Girls became more diverse. During the war, Navajo, Hopi, Zuni, and other Indian women were hired as were Hispanic women. Previously they had not been.

Doing Your Part

In 1943, Harvey Houses and dining cars prepared and served more than a million meals a month.[24] Food rationing, untrained employees, and the sheer numbers of service personnel that had to be fed put the company to the test. Inevitably, the consistency and quality of the meals and service declined. Some Harvey Houses and dining cars were as excellent as they always had been. But many others could not meet the same standards.

The company was cognizant of the problem and began running a series of ads in national magazines to counteract it. The ads focused on a mythical, and never pictured, Private Pringle. They asked for patience and understanding on the part of civilians as the company took care of the military personnel. If a passenger had to wait longer for a meal or had fewer food choices, it was all a part of the war effort. A typical ad showed a "Do Not Disturb" sign and the headline, "Shhhh! Private Pringle's Asleep." The ads also encouraged readers to conserve food, buy bonds, and pay necessary taxes without complaint.[25]

Other companies ran similar campaigns. Dining car menus exhorted passengers to support the war effort by buying savings bonds or taking their change in savings stamps. Ads sponsored by the Railroad Association called trains "The Old Reliable" and noted that they hauled five million tons of freight a day to meet the "demands of Defense." Menus and other literature reminded passengers that military personnel had priority. A New York Central ad urged patience and noted that the railroad was now serving "a meal a minute," or "3,000,000 EXTRA meals a year."[26]

A *20th Century* menu spelled out the new realities for passengers:

WARTIME
DINING CAR SERVICE

More diners . . . but no more dining cars.
More meals to serve . . . but less of many important foods to go around.
That is the wartime dining car situation.
. . .
This is why we are asking you to kindly leave the diner promptly when you have finished your meal in order that others may be served.
. . .
That is why some peacetime niceties are omitted . . . why meals are simplified to speed service . . . and why menus are planned to make the most of rationed foods.
. . .
From now till Victory we will go on serving you to the best of our ability. In the meantime, thanks for your aid and understanding in today's difficult situation.

The menu also noted that service personnel on furlough, traveling at their own expense, would be given a 10 percent reduction in the cost of their meals.

To take some of the pressure off the dining cars, the New Haven Railroad opened box lunch bars at Boston's South Station and New York's Grand Central Terminal. Simple plywood booths on wheels, the bars were staffed by the Grill Car Girls. The box lunches consisted of chicken salad or ham-and-pickle sandwiches, a small bottle of milk, and a piece of fruit.[27]

The United Service Organization (USO) set up canteens at many stations and gave the servicemen sandwiches, freshly baked cookies, cakes, and coffee. The soldiers had so little time that at many stations they couldn't even get off the train to get the food. Photographs show soldiers hanging out of train windows to take sandwiches from the volunteers. Thousands of volunteers made this work their contribution to the war effort. According to one USO estimate, more than six million individuals benefitted from these services.[28]

The New Haven Railroad commissioned copywriter Nelson Metcalfe Jr. to create its wartime messages. His campaign, "The Kid in Upper 4," became a classic:

It is 3:42 AM on a troop train. Men wrapped in blankets are breathing heavily. Two in every lower berth. One in every upper. This is no ordinary trip. It may be their last in the U.S.A. till the end of the war. Tomorrow they will be on the high seas. One is wide awake . . . listening . . . staring into the blackness. It is the kid in Upper 4. Tonight, he knows, he is leaving behind a lot of little things—and big ones. The taste of hamburgers and pop . . . the feel of driving a roadster over a six-lane highway . . . a dog named Shucks, or Spot, or Barnacle Bill. The pretty girl who writes so often . . . that gray-haired man, so proud and awkward at the station . . . the mother who knits the socks he'll wear soon. Tonight he's thinking them over. There's a lump in his throat. And maybe—a tear fills his eye. It doesn't matter, Kid. Nobody will see . . . it's too dark. A couple thousand miles away, where he's going, they don't know him very well. But people all over the world are waiting, praying for him to come. And he will come, this kid in Upper 4. With new hope, peace, and freedom for a tired, bleeding world.

Next time you are on the train, remember the kid in Upper 4. If you have to stand en route—it is so he may have a seat. If there is no berth for you, it is so that he may sleep. If you have to wait for a seat in the diner—it is so he . . . and thousands like him . . . may have a meal they won't forget in the days to come. For to treat him as our most honored guest is the least we can do to pay a mighty debt of gratitude.[29]

Everyone was doing his or her part. Railroad personnel in particular did exemplary work coping with rationing, mollifying regular passengers, and feeding the overwhelming number of troops. But their efforts may have actually contributed to the railroads' demise. After the war, many people—military and civilian alike—remembered the crowds, hasty service, less appetizing meals, and scheduling delays more than the need for the war effort or the dedication and hard work of the crews. Years later, a railroad executive speculated that the troop train experience hastened the downfall of the railroad after the war.[30]

Chafing Dish Recipes

Chafing dishes date back centuries. However, it's unlikely that Napoleon Bonaparte cooked omelets for Josephine in one, as Fannie Farmer claimed in the 1904 edition of her book, *Chafing Dish Possibilities*. Farmer thought chafing dishes had a special appeal for men. She wrote, "The bachelor feels himself proud to be called the pioneer in the use of this utensil." Years later a Fannie Farmer cookbook noted, "Many a man enjoys preparing a chafing dish specialty for guests." Farmer also claimed it was a useful utensil for a family on the maid's night off.

In more recent eras, their attractive appearance made chafing dishes popular for entertaining, buffets, and tableside cooking. When the New Haven Railroad added copper chafing dishes presided over by a buffet chef to its dining options in 1940, lobster Newburg was a popular choice. This is Fannie Farmer's recipe.

∾ *Lobster à la Newburg*

Remove the meat from a 2-pound lobster, and cut in slices or cubes. Melt ¼ cup butter, add the lobster, and cook until thoroughly heated. Season with ½ teaspoon salt, a few grains cayenne, a slight grating nutmeg, and 1 tablespoon each sherry wine and brandy. Cook one minute, and add ⅓ cup thin cream and the yolks of 2 eggs slightly beaten. Stir until sauce is thickened. Serve with toast or puff pastry points.

—Fannie Farmer, *Chafing Dish Possibilities*, 1904

Welsh Rarebit or Is It Rabbit?

Whether it's served as a simple dish of cheese on toast or a fancy chafing dish supper, Welsh *rarebit* originated as *rabbit*. Hannah Glasse's 1747 *Art of Cookery Made Plain and Easy* included recipes for Welsh, Scottish, and English rabbits. Her recipes are little more than toasted bread with cheese. She soaked the bread in red wine for her English version. But beer is usually the preferred beverage, both to be mixed with the cheese and drunk along with the dish. By the nineteenth century, the English and Scottish versions had all but disappeared, and the name had changed to Welsh rarebit, although some still kept the earlier usage.

Canned Welsh rarebit was popular—and served on trains—in the first half of the twentieth century. During the 1950s, when chafing dishes were enjoying a resurgence, homemade Welsh rarebit, or rabbit, became popular. This version is from a pamphlet that was issued by a now-defunct company that manufactured copperware including chafing dishes. It can be made in a chafing dish, if you have one, or a simple pot. Gruyere is a good change from cheddar cheese. Many cooks add a teaspoonful of Worcestershire sauce and/ or a splash of hot sauce.

∾ Welsh Rarebit

Serves 6

1 tablespoon butter
1 pound chopped Cheddar cheese
1 cup beer or ale
½ teaspoon paprika
½ teaspoon dry mustard
Dash of salt

With top pan set in water jacket, melt butter, and add cheese. While it is melting, slowly stir in the beer. Add seasonings. Stir constantly, with wooden spoon, until the mixture is blended and the cheese has melted. Serve at once on buttered toast.

—Coppercraft Guild, Inc., *32 Favorite Chafing Dish Recipes*, n.d.

CHAPTER 7

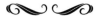

Endings and Beginnings

When Cary Grant and Eva Marie Saint dined aboard the *20th Century Limited* in Alfred Hitchcock's 1959 *North by Northwest*, they epitomized glamour and sophistication, as did their surroundings. Grant ordered a Gibson—more impressive than the usual martini. Saint recommended the brook trout. The dining table was set with snowy linens and fine china. There were fresh flowers in a silver vase. The server was quiet and unobtrusive. True, Grant and Saint were more interested in each other than in the meal, but it depicted a splendid moment for dining on the railroad.

However, it was one of the last and something of an illusion. The *20th Century* was nearing its end. A year earlier, coaches had been added to the once exclusively Pullman train. As a result, its reputation plummeted. Beebe, who had sung its praises loudly for years, lamented that its dining car service "was the first and most widely deplored manifestation of the new order of things." He did more than complain. He switched his allegiance to the *Century*'s rival, the Pennsylvania Railroad's *Broadway Limited*.

The Postwar Era

After the war many U.S. railroads built new cars and introduced new dining cars in what Karl Zimmerman, author of *20th Century Limited*, called "The American railroads' last, heroic, probably misguided attempt to impress and woo the rail traveler."[1]

THE *New* 20ᵀᴴ CENTURY LIMITED

NEW YORK - *16 hours* - CHICAGO

NEW YORK CENTRAL SYSTEM

Both the train and its memorable poster were the epitome of streamlined sophistication, however short-lived it would prove to be. Courtesy of the Bridgeman Art Library

The new *20th Century Limited* dining cars debuted in 1948. They were again designed by Henry Dreyfuss and included such features as magical fluorescent lighting and mirrored walls to make the area seem larger. The seating was angled in such a way that diners could look out at the passing scenery without looking directly across to diners at the opposite table. Electric eye doors eased passage from one car to another. The kitchen was now equipped with a freezer for ice creams and frozen food. The refrigerator had separate storage areas for seafood and dairy. There were even ice cube makers.

However, in a 1948 article about the cars titled "New Hopes & Ancient Rancors," *Time Magazine* waxed skeptical about the "mechanical marvel." After listing many of the inadequacies of rail travel—from stale tobacco smoke to frequent stops to erratic air conditioning—the article concluded with observations that were likely what the average American was thinking as well:

> There were radios in every room, built-in nurseries, movie theaters, lounge cars with Astra Domes, and trim hostesses. Were these wonders for him, or just for the cross-the-country glamor trade? Would he still have to stand in line 20 minutes or more for a seat in the diner? Would trains still lurch like wounded moose on jolting roadbeds? Perhaps what the passenger really wanted was less fluorescent and chromium luxury and more plain, old-fashioned convenience and comfort.[2]

The *20th Century*'s always renowned dining service continued to set standards in the 1950s with high-quality, but familiar, fare. A typical 1954 dinner menu offered relishes including olives, "celery farcie," radish rosettes, and spiced melon rind. Scattering a few French words around a menu was usual at the time, though listing plain old stuffed celery as "celery *farcie*" was particularly pretentious. In addition to the relishes, diners could begin with shrimp cocktail, crab bisque, consommé, or tomato juice. There were six main courses on the menu:

Filet of Fresh Gaspe Salmon Saute, Meuniere, Cucumbers
Buttered Zucchini, Baked Stuffed Potato

Roast Long Island Duckling, Celery Dressing, Bigarade
Minted Green Peas, Persillade Potatoes

Calf's Liver on Canadian Bacon, 20th Century
With Button Mushrooms and Fines Herbes Sauce
Garden Vegetable, Potatoes Hashed Browned Lyonnaise

Roast Ribs of Beef, Natural Gravy
Cauliflower Polonaise, Potatoes du Jour

Lamb Chops Grille, Pineapple Glace
Minted Green Peas, Baked Stuffed Potato

Charcoal Broiled Selected Sirloin Steak
(Button Mushrooms included on request)
Buttered Zucchini, Potatoes Hashed Browned Lyonnaise

Bigarade sauce is a classic accompaniment to duckling that owes its origins to famed eighteenth-century chef Antonin Carême. It's an *Espagnole*, or brown sauce, flavored with the zest and juice of bigarade, or bitter oranges. Menu prices ranged from $4.00 for the salmon to $5.85 for the steak. Desserts included "Old Fashioned Peach Shortcake, Whipped Cream," coconut pudding, chilled melon, and "N.Y.C. Special Ice Cream," as well as a variety of cheeses served with Ry-Krisp or crackers.[3]

In the 1950s, women, called "Girls of the Century," worked on the train wearing skirt suits designed by the famed Christian Dior. Their duties included giving travel talks, typing letters for traveling executives, and warming babies' bottles. The job required a college education.[4]

Despite the railroad's best efforts, the *20th Century* and railroads in general were on the decline. In 1958, in an article titled "Flying Is for the Birds," the noted church historian, author, and railroad fan Dr. Jaroslav Pelikan described the *20th Century* as being "of happy but now lamented memory." Although he disliked flying and called a plane little more than a "flying bus," Pelikan believed the railroads had let their standards slip. It is not coincidental that this was the year the *Century* added coaches. Echoing Beebe, Pelikan wrote: "Much as one might wish that the trains could capture the imagination of Americans again, it seems impossible. What is more, they are not even trying." Still committed to traveling by train whenever he could, he wrote that the "dining car remains a wondrous place to see and to smell." But he knew that its quality was waning. He wrote:

> A generation of travelers is rising now who may never know how good a meal en route can be. The salad bowl on the New York Central, the wheat cakes on the Wabash, the baked potato on the Great Northern, the whitefish on the Canadian Pacific—these are truly patrician. Or at least they used to be. On a railroad as in a marriage, the cuisine is one of the first things to suffer when times of trouble come.[5]

In the 1950s, many railroads cut back drastically on food service or eliminated it altogether because they couldn't afford the losses. Some rail lines tried replacing dining cars with bar cars. Members-only club or bar cars had been in service on railroads since the late nineteenth century, but in 1953, the New Haven started running bar cars for regular passengers. They were an especially big hit on the trains leaving Grand Central Station for the New York suburbs at the end of the workday, with some commuters enjoying three or four drinks on the ride home. Bartenders on the cars poured drinks from single-serving cans or nip bottles to control portion size, according to Marc

Frattasio, author of *Dining on the Shore Line Route*. The single-serve size also prevented railroad employees from pouring drinks for themselves. Boston commuters generally drank rye and ginger ale highballs. New York City commuters drank S.S. Pierce bourbon, Bell's Scotch, and Heublein premixed cocktails.[6]

The Heublein Company had introduced bottles of premixed, aged cocktails in the mid-nineteenth century. In the early years, they advertised them as being perfect "For the Yacht, Camping Party, Summer Hotel, Fishing Party, Mountains, Sea-Shore, or the Picnic." The ads went on to warn, "Avoid Imitations. Sold by Dealers generally, and on the Dining and Buffet Cars of the principal railroads."[7] By the 1960s, the list of cocktails had expanded to include vodka martinis, stingers, and daiquiris as well as Manhattans, whiskey sours, old-fashioneds, and sidecars. By then the ads read, "These are the famous cocktails served on leading airlines and railroads."[8]

Peanuts and cocktails turned out to be more profitable for the railroads than roast beef and claret. The New Haven's food service operation actually made a tiny profit of four cents on the dollar in 1961. But it was not enough. That was also the year the New Haven went bankrupt for the second time. On January 1, 1969, the New Haven Railroad was absorbed by the ill-fated Penn Central Transportation Company.[9]

Meal-a-Mat vending machines were another futile attempt by the railroads to cope with losses. The New York Central introduced them with some fanfare in October 1963 by having famed actress of the day Hermione Gingold demonstrate how easy it was for passengers to use the do-it-yourself "Radar Oven" to cook their own meals. Choices included "Macaroni au Gratin," "Broiled Salisbury Steak," "Roast Vermont Turkey" with dressing, and even "Lobster Newburg." Sandwiches, waffles, cookies, and other foods were also available from the machines. The railroad's publications touted the speed, convenience, and low prices of the new service. "Using microwave energy, the oven cooks the food thoroughly and at great speed," the railroad's "Headlight" newsletter pointed out. Entrees cooked in two minutes and forty-five seconds. The prices were right, even if the rest of the concept was not. Macaroni au gratin cost just seventy-five cents. The lobster Newburg was only $1.25. The Central called Meal-a-Mat its "newest economy travel star."[10]

Reaction from the press was less enthusiastic. Most news reports noted regretfully that machines, paper plates, and plastic utensils were taking the place of white-jacketed waiters, china, and silver. An article in the *Utica Daily Press* was headlined, "Central Replaces Sterling with Nickel." The article pointed out that the new cars eliminated the jobs of two dining car employees. All that was needed in the Meal-a-Mat car was an attendant who kept the machines stocked and served drinks. [11]

Most articles did admit that the railroads had been losing money on dining cars. New York's *Nunda News* quoted a New York Central spokesman as saying that the railroad had spent $1.28 for every dollar taken in by its dining cars the previous year. But, the article pointed out, "The Automatic Buffets don't make money, either. They've only shaved the dining car loss from $2.7 million in 1961 to $2.6 million last year."[12]

The *St. Petersburg Times* reported that other railroads were also trying automated service. "Southern Pacific, one of the more successful railroads in the country, lost $2,650,000 last year on its dining car service," reporter Thomas Rawlins wrote. Describing the Meal-A-Mat service, he explained, "Where it once took a chef, a waiter in charge and a waiter to man the costly kitchen, an attendant is now the sole traveling employee in the dining car. And the passengers do the cooking." Rawlins predicted, "The railroad dining car may soon go the way of the black, wood-stoked locomotive, a victim of economy-minded automation."[13]

Neither vending machines nor bar cars could save the beleaguered dining cars. Nothing could stem the tide.

The Holdouts: Beebe and Clegg

From 1946 to 1953, railroad passenger losses quintupled nationwide, according to Zimmerman.[14] Given the resulting cutbacks in service and the speed of the new airplanes, it's no wonder that passengers increasingly chose airlines. Even the most devoted rail fans were giving up on the grand world of rail travel, but Lucius Beebe and Charles Clegg defied the common wisdom and bought another private varnish car. They were among the last to do so and, for a brief moment, they owned two private cars. Their original car, *The Gold Coast*, had begun to show its age so, in 1954, they decided to donate it to the Pacific Coast Chapter of the Railway & Locomotive Historical Society at Oakland, California. However, they kept it until they acquired *The Virginia City* from the Pullman Company just so they could boast that they owned two private cars at the same time.[15]

Robert Hanley of Hollywood, who designed the lavish sets for *Auntie Mame* and many other films, redecorated *The Virginia City*'s interior at a cost of more than $375,000.[16] Beebe called the style Venetian Baroque. The draperies were gold silk, the fireplace was Italian marble, the chandeliers were Murano glass. There was even a steam room. In his book *Mansions on Wheels*, published in 1959, Beebe good-naturedly quoted an article written about the men and their car by the famed columnist for the *San Francisco Chronicle*, Herb Caen. The article began, "GILDED CAGE DEPT.: Fellow peasant, let me tell you how the rich people are living." Caen wrote that *The Virginia City* was the only truly private railway car left in the country. Quoting Clegg, Caen explained that the owners made no pretense to its being an office or business car. He wrote:

> "It's for pleasure only," says Mr. Clegg and to prove it mixed Martinis in the drawing room bar and we then walked into the dining room for lunch prepared by Wallace, the chef, and served by Clarence, the steward (both hires from the Southern Pacific). Nice little lunch. A creole fish soup with rice, Southern fried chicken, ham and beans, hot cornbread, pumpkin pie, a fine dry Bollinger champagne. "Wallace always prepares a light lunch," said Mr. Beebe. "You should stay for dinner. He's cooking a cow."

But even Clegg and Beebe knew the golden era of private varnish had ended. Beebe wrote its eulogy:

> So drew to a close the age of the most glamorous property of the once glamorous railroads, themselves now fallen upon a blighted age. But for a time the private railroad car all green and gold and glory had carried the nabobs to continental destinies and on far landfarings. They had been incomparably the symbol of an exalted social order and a bold philosophy of acquisition and possession. And they will be a part of the remembered epic of the American way of life forever.[17]

In Europe

The trains of the *Orient Express* resumed service after the war, but recovery took time. When the railroads did come back, they were not the same. The cars were not as grand, nor as well staffed. Some routes changed as a result of Iron Curtain politics. Sometimes just one sleeper was attached to a local train, which meant frequent stops and slow, tedious journeys. Trains often ran without any dining cars. It was not until 1952 that a through train ran from Paris to Istanbul via Salonika again. Airlines, not railways, had become the glamorous, and often less expensive, way to travel in the 1950s.

The novel *From Russia with Love*, written by Ian Fleming in 1956, took place in part on the *Orient Express*. Ever the romantic, Fleming wrote that the train "thunders superbly over the 1,400 miles of glittering steel track between Istanbul and Paris," which sounds impressive. But Fleming had to concede that James Bond was not traveling on the glamorous first-class-only train of the early twentieth century. Fleming wrote that there was now a "cheap half" attached to the train and "a chattering horde of peasants with bundles and wicker baskets" waited to board it at a station in the Balkans, at one of the many stops the train made. There was no restaurant car on the train at the beginning of the trip, and after one was attached in Yugoslavia, breakfast in the restaurant car consisted of "fried eggs and hard brown bread and coffee that was mostly chicory." The food improved when the train reached Trieste where Bond and the lovely Tatiana Romanova enjoyed *tagliatelle verdi* (spinach pasta) and "a delicious escalope," along with *Chianti Broglio,* and Romanova worried that eating such good food would make her fat. But even in fiction this was not the storied train of the past.[18]

Time Magazine reported that in 1960 the *Orient Express* had carried an average of one and a half passengers per trip on the line between Vienna and Bucharest, which led to its elimination. The *Simplon Orient Express*, which *Time* called "the slicker upstart," would continue to deliver its passengers efficiently, but "without the luxury their grandfathers had known."[19] Two years later, the magazine reported that luxury rail travel still existed, but it was now to be found in West Germany and in Japan. "U.S. railroads today would far rather haul freight than people—and they show it," reported *Time,* and the "glamorous *Orient Express,* beloved by mystery writers, has been curtailed." But the magazine had high praise for West Germany's *Rheingold Express* with its air-conditioned compartments and glass-walled observation car "for Rhineland castle watching," as well as its "cocktail lounge and gourmet restaurant." *Time* was also enthusiastic about Japan's high-speed trains with their "uniformed girls trundling carts richly laden with food and sake up and down the aisles."[20]

Many train aficionados rued and wrote about the decline of the grand old days of the *Orient Express,* but none more poignantly than Joseph Wechsberg. An author, musician, food writer, and train buff, in 1950 he wrote an article for the *New Yorker* on the sad state of the train. He remarked on the cracked mirror over the washbasin, the drafty windows, the watery soup. On the first leg of his trip there was a dining car and a menu that consisted of "*Omelette à la Turque, escalope à la Milanaise, pommes mousseline, choux-fleurs Polonaise, crème de Gruyère, pomme.*" When a fellow passenger, who was French, read the menu he complained, "My God, you'd think they were running a United Nations *bistro.*" Although the menu was not comprised of regional specialties, as it would have been in the past, Wechsberg said the dinner was good.

The Frenchman had left the train by the time the dining car had been taken off. Had he still been there he would have been even more disgruntled, since there was so little to eat. The dining car attendant managed to find a couple of rolls filled with garlic sausage and a small bottle of vodka for

Wechsberg. As they talked, the attendant mentioned that he had a daughter in the United States. He couldn't afford to visit her since his salary was low and tips at the time were few and meager, so he suggested Wechsberg might meet her if he went to Syracuse, New York, some day. However, he said, "Don't tell her what's happened to the *Orient Express*, though. Why destroy an illusion, Monsieur? Let her go on thinking her papa is an important man on an elegant, wonderful train—a real *train de mystère*."[21]

Years later, Wechsberg wrote a moving account titled "Last Man on the *Orient Express*" for the *Saturday Review* magazine. It began:

> It was 8:20 p.m. on the evening of Saturday, May 27, 1961. In a few minutes, the *Orient Express*, once a great train of romance and mystery, glamour and nostalgia, would leave for its last run from Paris to Bucharest . . . a great era in railroad history was coming to a close.

Again, Wechsberg described a shabby train, without a dining car for part of the way, lumbering along slowly and stopping frequently because it was hauling local trains and because soldiers conducted searches of the cars and passengers' luggage at border crossings. The few passengers onboard did not include the mysterious spies or *femmes fatales* of yesteryear, according to Wechsberg. Rather, he said that the young women looked as wholesome as toothpaste models. At the stations, unshaven men and peasant women carrying cardboard boxes tied with string waited to board the local cars. "A less glamorous crowd could hardly be imagined," Wechsberg wrote, "Hercule Poirot would have turned away in disgust."

Later in the trip, after a dining car had been attached, its headwaiter commiserated with Wechsberg about the train's fall from grace and showed him a menu dated June 5, 1903. "That day—the twentieth anniversary of the *Orient Express*—the passengers in the dining car had been offered *foie gras, saumon fumé, oeufs à la gelée, sole Metternich, poulet en cocotte,* followed by dessert, cheese, coffee," Wechsberg wrote. He quoted the headwaiter: "And now we're serving *Zwiebelrostbraten*. It's quite a letdown, isn't it?"

Zwiebelrostbraten is a homely Austrian dish of steak and fried onions. While it may be a much-loved comfort food, it is far from the haute cuisine served in that earlier day. Wechsberg concluded by writing, "The *Orient Express* was overtaken by the march of events and the speed of the airplane. Long before its last run it had become an anachronism." As if to prove his point, the magazine was filled with airline ads promoting the speed of air travel and the delights of destinations from London to Rome, from Beirut to Teheran.[22]

Various other Wagons-Lits trains continued to run for a few more years, but on May 19, 1977, the last through train ran from Paris to Istanbul. The train was made up of a sleeping car that had seen better days, and three coaches. There was no dining car. Passengers brought their own food or bought whatever was available at stations along the route. The train arrived in Istanbul five hours late.

Later that year in Monaco, Sotheby's auctioned off the Wagon-Lits rolling stock. If everyone who expressed sadness at the news of the last voyage of the fabled train had traveled on it more frequently in the preceding years, perhaps they would not have witnessed its demise. The airlines had proved to be too much competition for elite long distance rail travel. Most people preferred to spend a few hours in the air rather than a few days on the rails. In addition, the quality of rail service had deteriorated so much during the war and in the postwar years that some scarcely remembered the glory days of rail travel when fine dining and luxurious surroundings were taken for granted. Even if they did remember, when they had to be in Chicago/Paris/Rome by Tuesday/Wednesday/Thursday, they could not, or would not, take the time to take the train.

In its early years, air travel was as exciting and glamorous as rail travel had been in the late nineteenth century. Air passengers dressed up for their trips. In fact, some families dressed in their Sunday best to go to an airport and just watch planes take off. Stewardesses were glamorous creatures and pilots were heroes of the day. Pelikan, writing at a time when airlines were noted for their high service standards, praised them and said that railroads valued freight over passengers and treated them accordingly. He wrote, "The iron horse has become a nag."[23]

As U.S. railroads declined, went bankrupt, or threatened to do so, the passenger train seemed to be an endangered species. But many people still depended on, and some preferred, rail service. In 1970, President Richard Nixon signed the Rail Passenger Service Act into law to ensure the continuation of rail service. Originally called Railpax, its name was later changed to Amtrak. Some railroads did continue to operate privately but most joined Amtrak. Always subject to political controversy over costs and subsidies, Amtrak does not and was never intended to offer passengers the sort of grand dining experiences of the golden era of railroad travel.

Similarly, although some English and European railroads continue to offer luxury sleeping and dining car services, many have cut back or curtailed such services due to their high costs. Many passengers say they prefer rail travel; however, few are willing to pay the price it actually entails to enjoy it.

Remembrance of Trains Past

In the late nineteenth century, when railroads were supplanting horse-drawn carriages as a means of transportation, groups of people in England and in the United States took up driving the carriages as a hobby. They formed or reinvigorated associations often called Four-in-Hand clubs because the carriages were drawn by four horses and controlled by one driver. Earlier, when the horse-drawn carriages were strictly transportation, the drivers were working-class folk who earned their living by taking people to their destinations. When driving the carriages became a pastime, the drivers were no longer workers. They were men and sometimes women who were well off enough to be able to afford horses, carriages, and their upkeep. They also had the leisure time to indulge in the sport. In some instances, the clubs were popular enough to have an impact on local businesses. Some of the inns along the roads the carriages traveled saw increased activity as groups stopped for refreshments for themselves and their horses. The clubs turned what had been a practical form of transportation into a romantic recreational sport for those who could afford it.[24]

Often when a new technology takes over, the old becomes treasured. After newer methods of transportation such as automobiles and planes took the place of most train travel, particularly for long distances, nostalgia for the grand old days of railroading inspired some people to collect railroad memorabilia and to ride trains for pleasure and amusement rather than transportation.

Today rail enthusiasts, sometimes fondly referred to as *trainiacs*, ride on or dine in trains not to travel to a place, but simply to enjoy the experience of being on a train. Trains have become an end rather than a means to an end. They are a destination in themselves. Called heritage, tourist, or preserved railways, most of them are maintained with the intention of preserving railroad tradition. Some are, literally, museum pieces.

Train Museums

A website titled railmuseums.com lists 295 railway museums in North America, including nine in British Columbia, twenty-four in California, and three in Newfoundland. Internationally, there are seventy-two museums, with eighteen each in Europe and Australia and twenty in the United Kingdom.

Some museums, of course, are more extensive than others; many are run entirely by volunteers. Many offer short train rides along with the displays.

In addition to a myriad of locomotives, museum holdings may include dining cars, railroad china, scale model railroad cars, rail company uniforms, posters, tickets, timetables, toy trains, and even royal coaches. Many museums run educational programs and activities as well.

The "Palaces on Wheels" collection is the pride of the National Railway Museum in York, England, one of the world's largest rail museums. The palaces are a collection of carriages built for British royalty beginning with Queen Victoria. The museum's other holdings include nearly two million photographs documenting the history of railroading.[25]

The California State Railroad Museum in Sacramento features more than twenty restored locomotives and railroad cars, a reconstruction of a late nineteenth century passenger station, and exhibits dramatizing the ways the railroad influenced the development of the United States. It runs excursions in restored cars such as the *El Dorado*, a 1920s era Southern Pacific observation lounge car. For those who can't go to the museum or can't go there often enough, the museum, in partnership with the California State Library, the Sacramento Archives and Museum Collection Center, and the Sacramento Library, maintains a website (www.sacramentohistory.org) that illustrates the history of agriculture and transportation in the Sacramento Valley region from the mid-nineteenth century to the late 1920s.[26]

Theme Engines

In a nod to the fine dining of railways of the past, many short excursion trains offer food and wine in the elegant setting of restored dining cars. Some excursion trains are associated with museums; others are run independently, again often by volunteers. Train trips built around a variety of dining themes abound. In California's Napa Valley wine region, lovers of wine, food, and trains can combine their enthusiasms aboard restored dining cars as they enjoy scenic views of Napa vineyards. Often the train ride and meal are combined with a tour of a local winery, or built around a murder mystery theme, or a fall foliage tour. The meals are served aboard cars including a 1952 domed Pullman car, and feature the elegant service and table settings of yesteryear along with contemporary cuisine.[27]

On the other side of the country, a Newport, Rhode Island, dinner train offers meals aboard restored Pullman dining cars on a route along scenic Narragansett Bay. A special train, which the company calls "Rhode Island's only Moving Ice Cream Parlour Car," serves soft-serve ice cream sundaes and features entertainment by the "Candyman Conductor."[28]

The Strasburg Rail Road™ dining car at the station. Courtesy of the Strasburg Rail Road™

In Pennsylvania's Lancaster County visitors can ride on the Strasburg Rail Road™'s steam excursion trains amid Amish farmlands, dine in a first-class parlor car, visit the Railroad Museum of Pennsylvania, and stay in the Red Caboose Motel, which is made up of a collection of restored cabooses from lines such as the Union Pacific and the Lehigh Valley.

The Strasburg Rail Road™ takes visitors on a forty-five minute steam train ride, during which they can choose a dinner comprised of the traditional foods of the county, or a hobo's knapsack lunch presented by costumed servers, or other options. Children enjoy riding on a full-size steam locomotive that looks just like Thomas the Tank Engine, the much-loved star of a popular series of children's books. For a more grown-up treat, visitors can take part in the railroad's steampunk festival, featuring a Victorian-era dinner and an absinthe cocktail tasting.[29] Steampunk is a creative movement that celebrates the steam-powered machinery of the Industrial Revolution along with modern technology in a retro, futuristic, science fiction mash-up. Steam-powered trains are the perfect setting for steampunkers.

The Strasburg Rail Road™ wine and cheese car is always popular. Courtesy of the Strasburg Rail Road™

In England, as one would expect, there are many Afternoon Tea trains. Yorkshire's Bluebell Railroad serves afternoon tea aboard a beautifully restored *Golden Arrow* Pullman car. These cars once linked London and Paris in grand style. Today, full afternoon tea with a selection of teas, scones, cakes, sandwiches, and tarts is served on short scenic journeys in the Sheffield area. A railway museum is located at the restored Bluebell Station in Sheffield. The company also offers dinner trains, murder mystery trains, holiday and special celebration trains, and even an elegant private wedding breakfast train. The dinner trains depart at 7:30 p.m. and return at 11:00 p.m. These are typical *Golden Arrow* dinner menus:

Parsnip, Apple & Sage Soup
Wild Boar Terrine, Apricot & Ginger Chutney
Salmon & Dill Fishcake, Roasted Capsicum & Coriander Creme Fraiche
Roast Sirloin of Beef, Red Wine & Tarragon Jus
Venison & Roasted Root Vegetable Daube with Herb Dumpling
Halibut with a Sesame Seed & Chive Crust
Roasted Field Mushroom, Ratatouille Glazed with Local Golden Cross
    Goats Cheese

Apple & Blackberry Crumble Tartlet
Chocolate Profiteroles[30]

Other railways in the United Kingdom offer tea trains built around such themes as Alice in Wonderland's Mad Hatter tea, cream teas, steam teas, and Santa teas. The East Lancashire Railway offers excursions on weekends with lunch served in style aboard a restored steam-hauled Pullman dining car. The route goes through the scenic valleys and quaint villages of the Lancashire area. The beautifully appointed vintage cars boast wood paneling, crisp table linens, and fine china. These are sample menus for a three-course Sunday Lunch. Each one includes a vegetarian option.

Chicken liver paté with red onion relish
Tomato & mozzarella salad

Roast beef & Yorkshire pudding
Risotto stuffed peppers with tomato sauce & melting cheese

Banoffee pie [A banana and toffee pie]

Broccoli & cauliflower cheese soup

Roast leg of lamb with mint sauce & pan gravy
Roasted vegetable lasagna

Lemon meringue pie

Their Rail Ale Trail trains take ale fans to picturesque pubs and inns to sample classic British stouts, bitters, lagers, and ciders. There's even a stop at Mr. Fitzpatrick's in Rawtenstall, the country's oldest original temperance bar, where visitors can enjoy homemade sarsaparilla. Some of the pubs are located in or near restored rail stations.[31]

Private Varnish, Revised

Lucius Beebe would never have approved of considering a lowly caboose to be private varnish. The caboose was a humble car attached to the end of a freight train. It sheltered crew members responsible for switching and other duties, and might also serve as a galley, bunkroom, or an office for the conductor. Most cabooses have been phased out because of new technology and cuts in train staffing. But some have found new life.

A group of University of South Carolina football fans have turned twenty-two old cabooses into posh settings for private football tail—or rail—gating parties. The cars sit on an unused rail track close to the school's stadium and do not travel.

Over the years, the owners have decked out the thirty by nine foot cars with kitchens, baths, flat-screen televisions, air-conditioning, roof decks, and all sorts of other accouterments, much as owners of private cars did in years past. Collectively, the South Carolina cabooses are called the Cockaboose Railroad, after the university's varsity teams, known as Gamecocks. The tradition began in 1990 when a South Carolina businessman and football fan bought a retired caboose for a reported $10,000, fitted it up in style, and began hosting pre- and postgame parties in the car. Others followed his lead. The cockabooses are valued at up to $300,000 each, though the owners seldom part with them. Cockaboose parties have become a storied part of South Carolina football lore.[32]

Private varnish Beebe would have approved of has also returned. A few U.S. rail fans have bought old cars and renovated them. Like the private car owners of Beebe's era, the owners refurbish the cars to suit their own tastes and needs, with whatever configuration of stylish sleeping quarters, baths, kitchens, and dining areas they like. Reportedly, refurbishing a car can cost up to half a million dollars depending on the owners' whims. To help defray costs, some owners rent out their cars from time to time.

When the owners want to travel, they arrange to attach the car to an Amtrak train. Amtrak charges about two dollars a mile to pull a private car, as well as $100 a night for parking. There are also crew costs and the price of hauling a car from storage to the train. A trip from New York to Chicago can cost the private car owner from $2,000 to $3,000 depending on the number of crew and incidental costs. The same trip aboard the *Lake Shore Limited* costs from $100 for a value coach seat to $957 for a Viewliner Bedroom accommodation.

The private cars have to be attached to trains that travel no more than 110 miles per hour, according to federal law. Although private car passengers still have to endure the same frequent stops and freight car delays of the train they're attached to, traveling in a private car means eating when and whatever you like, not being awakened by station announcements, and having lots more room to stretch out in comfort. Since the private car is attached to the end of the train and usually has large windows, its passengers also enjoy wonderful views of the countryside as they ride.[33]

Some groups specialize in rail car rentals. An organization based in England, the Train Chartering Company Ltd., organizes private and luxury train travel for individuals and for organizations. Using refurbished cars from the early days of the twentieth century and the later Art Deco era, the company operates everywhere from the United States to the United Kingdom, from Morocco to Switzerland.

The cars are usually attached to regularly scheduled rail services and generally include dining and kitchen areas, bedrooms, lounges, and often observation domes. The private car rentals include chef and butler services and an extraordinary level of luxurious pampering. The company also charters entire trains, such as Spain's luxurious *El Transcantabrico* or South Africa's famed *Blue Train,* for groups who like to travel together in comfort and style.[34]

The Rebirth of the *Venice Simplon Orient-Express*

Lovers of old-style luxury train travel have managed to keep some of its finest cars alive and traveling. Various individuals and groups have built or restored luxury trains, but none have done it more successfully than James Sherwood.

An elegantly restored *Venice Simplon Orient-Express* dining car. Courtesy of the Venice Simplon Orient-Express Trains & Cruises

In 1977, Sotheby's auctioned off five of the *Venice Simplon Orient-Express* carriages, the ones that had been used in the filming of *Murder on the Orient Express*. James Sherwood, owner of the Sea Containers Group, went to the auction to see if he could find a bargain.

The auction attracted a lot of attention and was attended by swarms of people, some intent on bidding, others there simply to see the cars and the celebrities. Despite a publicity photograph of Princess Grace of Monaco having brunch in an elegant dining car designed by René Lalique, the carriages that looked so luxurious in the 1974 film had fallen on hard times. They needed to be completely restored.

The then king of Morocco bought two cars to add to his private train. Sherwood bought two sleeping cars. In her book, *Venice Simplon Orient-Express: The Return of the World's Most Celebrated Train*, Shirley Sherwood described her reaction when she saw the cars her husband had bought. "As I clambered in and out of derelict Pullmans with smashed windows and filthy marquetry I was secretly amazed that my husband felt something could be rescued from the mess."[35] Undeterred, during the next few years the Sherwoods located and bought other cars, including diners, to form a whole rake, or complete train in rail terms. If they were to run and carry passengers, rather than sit in a museum exhibit, the cars would have to be rebuilt to meet contemporary safety requirements. All the cars had to have their systems—from brakes to electricity to heating—updated.

To recapture the style and elegance the cars had lost, the Sherwoods needed to locate craftspeople who had the skills to replace or restore such decorative items as the mosaics for the floors of the lavatories, the inlaid marquetry for the wooden paneling in the cars, and the Lalique glass panels that decorated one of the dining cars. Sadly, some of the Lalique panels were stolen in the process and had to be replaced with new ones. The Sherwoods also had to tend to such details as replacing the flammable celluloid lampshades in the dining cars with safer pleated silk ones and reupholstering the furniture with flame-retardant, but period appropriate, fabrics. They found fine china, crystal, and linens in the style of the old trains to outfit the dining cars and hired an exceptional team to staff them. Like their predecessors, these dining cars were to offer elegant dining.

The new *Venice Simplon Orient-Express* was launched successfully on May 25, 1982. It has continued and expanded ever since, offering luxurious travel and fine dining. Its menus today are a combination of classic French cuisine and contemporary innovations. Dinners vary according to the seasons and destinations. This is an example of the cuisine enjoyed by its passengers.

Dining car service on one of the restored cars. Courtesy of the Venice Simplon Orient-Express Trains & Cruises

Le dîner

Turban de bar cuit au four, farci de pignons de pin et de tomates séchées, tuile de pain au pesto
Roasted seabass roulade with pine nuts and dried tomatoes filling
Pesto bread lace biscuit

Magret de canard des Landes rôti aux fèves de cacao épicées
Escalope de foie gras frais en "crumble"
Roasted Landes duck breast in spicy cocoa sauce
Pan fried duck foie gras in crusty crumble

Carottes fondantes au cumin
Buttered carrots with cumin

Croustillant de pommes de terre
Crispy potato pie

Sélection du maître fromager
Choice of finely selected cheeses

Soufflé au Grand Marnier
Grand Marnier soufflé

Mignardises
Small pastry delicacies

Café de Colombie
Colombian coffee

The shabby cars Sherwood bought at auction years ago were indeed rescued from the mess Shirley Sherwood first encountered. Lucius Beebe and Hercule Poirot would be impressed. The cars are as lavish and luxurious now as they were during the golden age of rail travel, the age that inspired so many novels and films.

It is true that traveling and dining in private rail cars or such trains as the restored *Venice Simplon Orient-Express* is beyond the means of the average person. But then it always was.

Banoffee Pie

This gooey pie, named for a play on the words "banana" and "toffee," was invented in 1972 for the dessert menu at an English pub called the Hungry Monk. A popular "pudding" on English menus ever since, it's served on the East Lancashire Railway's weekend excursion trains.

The heart of the pie—a chewy, fudgy, toffee filling made from sweetened condensed milk—is similar to the South American favorite *dulce de leche*. To make ahead of time, prepare the toffee filling and pour into the crust, cover, and refrigerate up to one day in advance. Before serving, top the pie with fresh banana slices and mound with whipped cream. Crumbly, whole meal English digestive biscuits make the best crust, but graham crackers work well, too.

A chef greets *Venice Simplon Orient-Express* passengers. Courtesy of the Venice Simplon Orient-Express Trains & Cruises

∽ *Banoffee Pie*

Yields: 6 to 8 servings

For the Filling:

  2 cans (14 ounces each) sweetened condensed milk
  1 teaspoon vanilla extract
  ¼ cup firmly packed, dark brown sugar
  4 tablespoons unsalted butter, melted
  ¼ teaspoon fine sea salt
  Boiling water (as needed)

For the Crumb Crust:

  2 cups whole meal digestive biscuit crumbs or graham cracker crumbs
  5 tablespoons granulated sugar
  ½ cup (1 stick) unsalted butter, melted

For the Topping:

    3 barely ripe bananas
    2 cups heavy cream
    ⅓ cup confectioners' sugar
    ¼ teaspoon instant espresso dissolved in 1 teaspoon pure vanilla extract

Preheat oven to 400 degrees.

To make the filling: Stir together the sweetened condensed milk, vanilla, brown sugar, melted butter, and salt. Pour into a 6-cup oven-proof dish and cover with aluminum foil. Place the dish in a 9-by-13-inch baking pan and fill the pan with boiling water until it reaches halfway up the sides of the dish. Bake the milk mixture, stirring every 15 minutes, until it is reduced and thickened and has turned a toasty caramel color, about 1½ to 2 hours. Remove from the oven and let cool. Reduce the oven temperature to 350 degrees.

While the filling is cooling, prepare the crumb crust: In a small bowl, combine the biscuit or graham cracker crumbs with the granulated sugar and melted butter. Stir together until the crumbs are completely moistened. Press them into a 9-inch tart pan 3 inches deep with a removable bottom, or a 9-inch pie pan. Bake just until crisp, about 5 to 7 minutes. Transfer to a wire rack to cool.

When the toffee filling has cooled slightly, but is still soft, spoon into the cooled crumb crust, spreading it in an even layer. Refrigerate the pie until the filling is set. You can cover the pie with plastic wrap and keep it chilled at this point for 24 hours.

To make the topping: Peel and slice the bananas into ½-inch thick slices and arrange them over the toffee. In a bowl, using an electric mixer set at medium speed, whip the cream with the confectioners' sugar and the espresso/vanilla flavoring until stiff peaks form. Pile the whipped cream on top of the bananas, spreading it toward the edges of the crust, making sure the fruit is completely covered to inhibit browning. Refrigerate the pie until ready to serve.

—From *Sticky, Chewy, Messy, Gooey: Desserts for the Serious Sweet Tooth* by Jill O'Connor. © Copyright 2007/Chronicle Books. Used with permission.

Afterword

Take the Train

Everyone I've spoken to about this book has said exactly the same thing: "I love trains." Then they say that they haven't taken a train, except a commuter train, in years. Or that they take trains in Europe but not in America. Or that they fondly remember traveling all over Europe on a Eurail pass when they were in college. That's usually said by people whose children are now in college. Some say they've taken a wine train in Napa or a scenic train in the Berkshires. But they do not actually travel on trains.

If people never travel on trains, I often wonder, how can they claim to *love* them? It's fine to ride on an excursion train or a dinner train or museum train. There's nothing wrong with that. But I suggest that the next time you take a vacation, you travel to your destination by train. It may take longer, but the train trip will be part of the vacation rather than simply something to be endured until you arrive. If you have children, they'll get a geography lesson they'll enjoy and never forget.

Trains give you a feel for a place, even if you're just passing through. When you see the coast of Connecticut from a train, you understand why it was a shipbuilding center. From a car or a plane, you do not. Riding on the train they call the *City of New Orleans* through the swamps and bayous of Louisiana and Mississippi makes clear why Hurricane Katrina wreaked such havoc on the area. When you see how flat the land is and how high the water, the landscape comes alive in a way that's different from a newspaper account or even a television image. We all know that Texas is big. Just how big is made evident when you travel its breadth on a train. The train speeds along, hour after hour, and never leaves the state.

You are more likely to meet and engage with people on a train than on a plane. Many of them will be train buffs who'll tell you about the features of various routes and the must-see stops along the way. You may meet people who actually live and work in the place you're visiting. An Italian family on the train from Rome to Pescara may turn out to have relatives in your hometown. On a train in Texas, you may meet Texans who'll tell you where to get the best Mexican food in San Antonio.

When you travel by train, you'll arrive in or near the center of a town, and you'll learn what the people of that town think about trains. Chicago's Union Station is glorious. It says, "Train travel matters here." Houston's train station is dismal. It says, "Nobody who is anybody takes the train." The people of Longview, Texas, bought their train depot from the Union Pacific Railroad, and they're raising funds to restore and expand it. That says it all.

Those Americans who believe in the superiority of the European experience might change their minds when they arrive at the station in Ravenna and have to lug their suitcases down a flight of stairs, under the tracks, and up a flight of stairs to make their way out of the station. Walking out across the tracks is strictly forbidden. However, if an attractive woman smiles and looks helplessly at her heavy suitcase, a handsome policeman will escort her across the tracks. And she will have learned a lesson in Italian ways.

Railways aren't perfect, anywhere. Don't expect grand accommodations every time you travel by train. Trains vary. Some are clean and comfortable. Others are not. Don't expect fine dining everywhere either. The food is usually better than airline food or fast food, but with the exception of the extremely posh high-end trains, it's not wonderful. High-speed trains seldom serve anything but snacks because they reach their destinations so quickly there's no time for real meals. Slower trains may or may not serve food.

You can't expect perfection from trains any more than you can expect it from your spouse or your kids. Like them, trains have their flaws and idiosyncrasies. If you travel on trains, you'll love them despite—or even for—their flaws. If you travel on trains, then you can say you *love* trains.

Notes

Introduction

1. John-Peter Pham, *Heirs of the Fisherman: Behind the Scenes of Papal Death and Succession* (London: Oxford University Press, 2006), 20–21.

2. Jules Janin, *The American in Paris* (Paris: Longman, Brown, Green and Longmans, 1843), 167, www.books.google.com (accessed April 25, 2013).

Chapter 1

1. Sir William Mitchell Acworth, *The Railways of England* (London: John Murray, 1889), 2–4.

2. Acworth, *Railways of England*, 45.

3. Charles Dickens, *The Uncommercial Traveller* (New York: President, n.d.), 48.

4. Anthony Trollope, *He Knew He Was Right* (London: Penguin Books, 1994), 316.

5. Chris de Winter Hebron, *Dining at Speed: A Celebration of 125 Years of Railway Catering* (Kettering: Silver Link, 2004), 16.

6. Acworth, *Railways of England*, 146.

7. David Burton, *The Raj at Table* (London: Faber and Faber, 1994), 45.

8. Thomas Cook, *Cook's Excursionist*, 28 August 1863. In *Oxford Dictionary of National Biography*, 2013, www.oup.com/oxforddnb/info (accessed April 5, 2013).

9. Michel Chevalier, *Society, Manners, and Politics in the United States* (New York: Cornell University Press, 1961), 11.

10. Charles MacKay, *Life and Liberty in America: Sketches of a Tour in the United States and Canada in 1857–1858* (London: Smith, Elder and Co., 1859), vi, www.books.google.com (accessed April 5, 2013).

11. Frederick Marryat, *A Diary in America, with Remarks on Its Institutions* (New York: Alfred A. Knopf, 1962), 366–68.

12. Marryat, *A Diary in America*, 369.

13. Ibid., 27–28.

14. E. Catherine Bates, *A Year in the Great Republic* (London: Ward & Downey, 1887), cited in August Mencken, *The Railroad Passenger Car: An Illustrated History of the First Hundred Years, with Accounts by Contemporary Passengers* (Baltimore: Johns Hopkins University Press, 1957), 186.

15. John Whetham Boddam-Whetham, *Western Wanderings: A Record of Travel in the Evening Land* (London: Spottiswoode and Co., 1874), 57–58.

16. Chevalier, *Society, Manners, and Politics in the United States*, 270.

17. Marryat, *A Diary in America*, 264.

18. University of Nevada, Las Vegas Digital Collections, http://digital.library.univ.edu (accessed April 12, 2013).

19. *Kansas City Star*, 1915, quoted in Lucius Beebe, "Purveyor to the West," *American Heritage Magazine*, Volume 18, Number 2 (February 1967), www.americanheritage.com (accessed May 6, 2013).

20. Mencken, *The Railroad Passenger Car*, 118–19.

21. Noel Coward, *Quadrille: A Romantic Comedy in Three Acts* (New York: Doubleday & Company, 1955), 136.

22. Robert Louis Stevenson, *The Amateur Emigrant* (Chicago: Stone & Kimball, 1895), cited in *We Took the Train*, ed. H. Roger Grant (DeKalb: Northern Illinois University Press, 1990), 57.

23. Michael Hamilton, *Down Memory Line* (Leitrim, Ireland: Drumlin, 1997), 93.

24. Marc Frattasio, *Dining on the Shore Line Route: The History and Recipes of the New Haven Railroad Dining Car Department* (Lynchburg, VA: TLC, 2003), 4.

25. Barbara Haber, *From Hardtack to Home Fries: An Uncommon History of American Cooks and Meals* (New York: The Free Press, 2002) 87–102.

26. Stephen Fried, *Appetite for America: How Visionary Businessman Fred Harvey Built a Railroad Hospitality Empire That Civilized the Wild West* (New York: Bantam Books, 2010), 94.

Chapter 2

1. Terence Mulligan, "The Delights of Pullman Dining USA 1866–1968" (Pullman Car Services Supplement Edition, April 2007), 5, www.semgonline.com (accessed April 9, 2013).

2. Henry James, *The American Scene* (New York: Harper & Brothers, 1907), 191.

3. Joseph Husband, *The Story of the Pullman Car* (Chicago: A.C. McClurg & Co., 1917), 49.

4. W.F. Rae, *Westward by Rail: The New Route to the East* (London: Longmans, Green, and Co., 1870), 28–30.

5. Rae, *Westward by Rail*, 30.

6. James Macaulay, *Across the Ferry: First Impressions of America* (London: Hodder and Stoughton, 1884), 137–38.

7. Macaulay, *Across the Ferry*, 142.

8. United States Patent Office, Patent No. 89,537, dated April 27, 1869, www.uspto.gov (accessed April 10, 2013).

9. John H. White Jr., *The American Railroad Passenger Car* (Baltimore: Johns Hopkins University Press, 1978), 316–17.

10. Lucy Kinsella, "Chicago Stories: Pullman Porters: From Servitude to Civil Rights," Window to the World Communications, www.wttw.com (accessed April 10, 2013).

11. "Spies on Pullman Cars," *The New York Times*, February 6, 1886, www.nytimes.com (accessed April 10, 2013).

12. Ellen Douglas Williamson, *When We Went First Class* (Garden City, NY: Doubleday, 1977), in *We Took the Train*, ed. H. Roger Grant (DeKalb: Northern Illinois University Press, 1990), 113.

13. Lucius Beebe and Charles Clegg, *The Trains We Rode* (Berkeley, CA: Howell-North Books, 1965–1966), 838.

14. Hill Harper, *The Wealth Cure: Putting Money in Its Place* (New York: Penguin Group, 2012), 118.

15. "Paderewski Chef Quits Pullman Job," *The New York Times*, January 3, 1928, www.nytimes.com (accessed April 10, 2013).

16. Railroad dining ware has become a desirable collectable and enthusiasts pay high prices for particular pieces. Since designs changed over time, collectors often specialize in an era as well as a specific railroad line.

17. "Across the Continent: From the Missouri to the Pacific Ocean by Rail," *The New York Times*, June 28, 1869; Central Pacific Railroad Photographic History Museum, www.cprr.org (accessed April 10, 2013).

18. Husband, *The Story of the Pullman Car*, 80.

19. T.S. Hudson, *A Scamper Through America or, Fifteen Thousand Miles of Ocean and Continent in Sixty Days* (London: Griffith & Farran, 1882), 83–84.

20. William A. McKenzie, *Dining Car Line to the Pacific* (St. Paul: Minnesota Historical Society Press, 1990), 68–74.

21. University of Nevada, Las Vegas, http://digital.library.univ.edu/objects/menus (accessed January 29, 2013).

22. The Union Oyster House in Boston was designated a National Historic Landmark in 2003. The oldest continually operated restaurant and oyster bar in the United States, it was constructed between 1716 and 1717. Its patrons have included such notables as Daniel Webster and President John F. Kennedy.

23. www.pullman-museum.org (accessed March 26, 2013).

24. Timothy Shaw, *The World of Escoffier* (New York: Vendome Press, 1995), 89.

25. Lucius Morris Beebe, Mr. Pullman's Elegant Palace Car (New York: Doubleday, 1961), 347.

26. Ibid., 123–24.

27. James D. Porterfield, Dining by Rail: The History and the Recipes of America's Golden Age of Railroad Cuisine (New York: St. Martin's Press, 1993), 55–60.

28. White, The American Railroad Passenger Car, 319.

29. Ibid., 311–20.

30. http://menus.nypl.org/menu (accessed April 24, 2013).

31. White, The American Railroad Passenger Car, 320.

32. American Magazine, Volume 85 (1918), 144. www.babel.hathatrust.org (accessed April 14, 2013).

33. Moses King, King's Handbook of New York City: An Outline History and Description of the American Metropolis (Boston: Moses King, 1892), 109.

34. http://menus.nypl.org/menu (accessed April 24, 2013).

Chapter 3

1. Jenifer Harvey Lang, ed., Larousse Gastronomique (New York: Crown Publishers, 1990), 1110.

2. E.H. Cookridge, Orient Express: The Life and Times of the World's Most Famous Train (New York: Random House, 1978), 34–38.

3. Lynne Withey, Grand Tours and Cook's Tours: A History of Leisure Travel, 1750–1915 (New York: William Morrow and Company, 1997), 181.

4. Anthony Burton, The Orient Express: The History of the Orient Express Service from 1883 to 1950 (Edison, NJ: Chartwell Books, 2001), 18–19.

5. "To Sunny Italy by the Rome Express: An Account of the First Journey by a Passenger," Railway Magazine, December 1897.

6. Burton, The Orient Express, 45–49.

7. "To Sunny Italy by the Rome Express."

8. Cookridge, Orient Express, 103.

9. George Behrend, Luxury Trains from the Orient Express to the TGV (New York: Vendome Press, 1982), 28.

10. Dictionary of Victorian London, www.victorianlondon.org (accessed May 21, 2013).

11. "Europe: Off Goes the Orient Express," Time Magazine, October 31, 1960, www.time.com (accessed May 21, 2013).

12. T.F.R. "The Pleasures of the Dining-Car," Railway Magazine, Volume 7 (July–December 1900), 520–21.

13. "To Sunny Italy by the Rome Express."

14. Philip Unwin, Travelling by Train in the Edwardian Age (London: George Allen & Unwin, 1979), 90.

15. Chris de Winter Hebron, Dining at Speed: A Celebration of 125 Years of Railway Catering (Kettering: Silver Link, 2004), 38–39.

16. Unwin, Travelling by Train in the Edwardian Age, 90.

17. Ibid., 51.

18. Joseph Husband, *The Story of the Pullman Car* (Chicago: A.C. McClurg & Co., 1917), 67.

19. "Pullman Dining Cars: A Trial Trip on the English Midland Railway," *The New York Times*, July 19, 1882, www.nytimes.com (accessed May 21, 2013).

20. Christian Wolmar, *Blood, Iron, and Gold* (New York: Public Affairs, 2010), 260–61.

21. Francis E. Clark, *The Great Siberian Railway: What I Saw on My Journey* (London: S.W. Partridge and Co., 1904), http://www.archive.org/stream/greatsiberianrai 00clariala/greatsiberianrai00clariala_djvu.txt (accessed March 12, 2013).

Chapter 4

1. Chris de Winter Hebron, *Dining at Speed: A Celebration of 125 Years of Railway Catering* (Kettering: Silver Link, 2004), 12.

2. Lynne Withey, *Grand Tours and Cook's Tours: A History of Leisure Travel 1750–1915* (New York: William Morrow, 1997), 314–15.

3. *Railway Magazine*, Volume 7 (July–December 1900), 520–21.

4. Roger H. Grant, *We Took the Train* (DeKalb: Northern Illinois University Press, 1990), xxiv.

5. Stephen Fried, *Appetite for America: How Visionary Businessman Fred Harvey Built a Railroad Hospitality Empire That Civilized the Wild West* (New York: Bantam Books, 2010), 392.

6. Lucius Morris Beebe, *Mr. Pullman's Elegant Palace Car* (New York: Doubleday, 1961), 13.

7. http://www.gngoat.org/17th_page.htm (accessed August 9, 2013).

8. Whithey, *Grand Tours and Cook's Tours*, 190.

9. George Moerlein, *A Trip Around the World* (Cincinnati: M&R Burgheim, 1886), 24–25.

10. New York Public Library Menu Collection, http://menus.nypl.org/menu_pages/10262 (accessed August 10, 2013).

11. Andrew Smith, *American Tuna: The Rise and Fall of an Improbable Food* (Berkeley: University of California Press, 2012), 21–35.

12. Lowell Edmunds, *Martini, Straight Up: The Classic American Cocktail* (Baltimore: Johns Hopkins University Press, 1998), xix.

13. Lucius Beebe, *Mansions on Rails: The Folklore of the Private Railway Car* (Berkeley, CA: Howell-North, 1959), 20–21.

14. Beebe, *Mansions*, 17.

15. Ibid., 205–6.

16. Ibid., 20.

17. Beebe, *Mr. Pullman*, 352.

18. Rufus Estes, *Good Things to Eat, As Suggested by Rufus* (Chicago: The Author, ca. 1911); Feeding America, http://digital.lib.mus.edu, 5–7.

19. Ibid., 68.

20. Ibid., 49–50.

21. Ibid., 8.

22. Ibid., 49–50.

23. Ibid., 21.

24. Ibid., 92.

25. Ibid., 40.

26. Ibid., 31–33.

27. Ibid., 38.

28. Ibid., 103–30.

Chapter 5

1. Harvey Levenstein, *Revolution at the Table: The Transformation of the American Diet* (New York: Oxford University Press, 1988), 141.

2. Christian Wolmar, *Blood, Iron and Gold* (New York: Public Affairs, 2010), 284.

3. Peter M. Kalla-Bishop and John W. Wood, *The Golden Years of Trains: 1830–1920* (New York: Crescent Books, in association with Phoebus, 1977), 98.

4. Wolmar, *Blood, Iron and Gold*, 284.

5. Kalla-Bishop and Wood, *The Golden Years of Trains*, 102.

6. Gay Morris, "Dance: 'Le Train Bleu' Makes a Brief Stopover," *The New York Times*, March 4, 1990, http://www.nytimes.com/1990/03/04/arts (accessed August 9, 2013).

7. Ibid.

8. "Foreign News: Orient Express," *Time*, April 29, 1935. www.time.com (accessed September 10, 2013).

9. W.M. Acworth, *The Railways of England* (London: John Murray, 1889), 231–32.

10. Shirley Sherwood, *Venice Simplon Orient-Express: The Return of the World's Most Celebrated Train* (London: Weidenfeld & Nicolson, 1983), 48–49.

11. Beverley Nichols, *No Place Like Home* (London: Jonathan Cape, 1936), 47.

12. Ibid., 55–56.

13. Malcolm W. Browne, "The 20th Century Makes Final Run," *The New York Times*, December 3, 1967. www.nytimes.com/archives (accessed September 19, 2013).

14. Karl Zimmerman, *20th Century Limited* (St. Paul, MN: MBI Publishing Company, 2002), 32.

15. Ibid., 54–56.

16. Lucius Beebe, *20th Century: The Greatest Train in the World* (Berkeley, CA: Howell-North, 1962), 82.

17. Michael L. Grace, "The Twentieth Century Limited," http:www.newyorksocialdiary.com (accessed September 10, 2013).

18. H. Roger Grant, *We Took the Train* (DeKalb: Northern Illinois University Press, 1990), xviii.

19. Chris de Winter Hebron, *Dining at Speed: A Celebration of 125 Years of Railway Catering* (Kettering: Silver Link, 2004), 79.

20. Ibid., 80

21. Jenifer Harvey Lang, ed., *Larousse Gastronomique* (New York: Crown, 1990), 393.

22. Western Pacific Railroad Dining Car Menu [19--], California State Railroad Museum Library. www.sacramentohistory.org (accessed September 26, 2013).

23. Andrew Smith, ed., *The Oxford Encyclopedia of Food and Drink in America* (New York: Oxford University Press, 2004), Volume 2, 32.

24. "3.2% Beer," National Institute on Alcohol Abuse and Alcoholism, http://alcoholpolicy.niaaa.nih.gov/3_2_beer_2.html (accessed September 25, 2013).

25. Levenstein, *Revolution at the Table*, 153, 197–98.

26. Marc Frattasio, *Dining on the Shore Line Route: The History and Recipes of the New Haven Railroad Dining Car Department* (Lynchburg, VA: TLC Publishing, 2003), 17.

27. Beebe, *20th Century*, 89.

28. "Streamliner Train: City of Denver," *Denver Post*, http://blogs.denverpost.com/library/2013/06/12/union-pacifics-city-of-denver-streamliner-train/8643/ (accessed September 26, 2013).

29. "Little Nugget," American Southwestern Railway Association, Inc., http://www.mcscom.com/asra/nugget.htm (accessed September 26, 2013).

30. Patricia Herlihy, *Vodka: A Global History* (London: Reaktion Books, 2012), 68–70.

31. Joseph M. Carlin, *Cocktails: A Global History* (London: Reaktion Books, 2012), 78–79.

32. Herlihy, *Vodka*, 78–79.

33. *Railway Age*, February 16, 1924, 76–77, www.foodtimeline.org/restaurants.html#childmenus (accessed August 15, 2013).

Chapter 6

1. John H. White Jr., *The American Railroad Passenger Car* (Baltimore: Johns Hopkins University Press, 1978), 341.

2. Ibid., 311–12.

3. H. Roger Grant, *We Took the Train* (DeKalb: Northern Illinois University Press, 1990), xiii.

4. Christian Wolmar, *Blood, Iron, and Gold* (New York: Public Affairs, 2010), 286.

5. White, *The American Railroad Passenger Car*, 357.

6. Karl Zimmerman, *20th Century Limited* (St. Paul, MN: MBI Publishing Company, 2002), 80.

7. White, *The American Railroad Passenger Car*, 320–38.

8. *Railway Gazette*, December 9, 1887, 796, www.books.google.com (accessed August 12, 2013).

9. Jerry Thomas, *How to Mix Drinks, or The Bon-Vivant's Companion* (New York: Dick & Fitzgerald, 1862), 105.

10. Lucius Morris Beebe, *Mr. Pullman's Elegant Palace Car* (New York: Doubleday, 1961), 269.

11. Chris de Winter Hebron, *Dining at Speed: A Celebration of 125 Years of Railway Catering* (Kettering: Silver Link, 2004), 51–75.

12. Ibid., 76.

13. Marc Frattasio, *Dining on the Shore Line Route* (Lynchburg, VA: TLC Publishing, 2003), 17–21.

14. H. Roger Grant, *Railroads and the American People* (Bloomington: Indiana University Press, 2012), 24.

15. William A. McKenzie, *Dining Car Line to the Pacific* (St. Paul: Minnesota Historical Society Press, 1990), 71–72.

16. Sacramento History Online, *Southern Pacific Bulletin*, www.sacramentohistory. org (accessed September 17, 2013).

17. E.H. Cookridge, *Orient Express: The Life and Times of the World's Most Famous Train* (New York: Random House, 1978), 102.

18. Pennsylvania Railroad, *The Pennsylvania Railroad Dining Car Department, Instructions*, 1938.

19. Frattasio, *Dining on the Shore Line Route*, 67.

20. Ibid., 32.

21. David P. Morgan, "Troop Train," in *We Took the Train*, ed. H. Roger Grant (DeKalb: Northern Illinois University Press, 1990), 143.

22. James D. Porterfield, *Dining by Rail: The History and Recipes of America's Golden Age of Railroad Cuisine* (New York: St. Martin's Press, 1993), 108–9.

23. Stephen Fried, *Appetite for America: How Visionary Businessman Fred Harvey Built a Railroad Hospitality Empire That Civilized the Wild West* (New York: Bantam Books, 2010), 370–72.

24. Lesley Poling-Kempes, *The Harvey Girls: Women Who Opened the West* (New York: Paragon House, 1989), 192–95.

25. Fried, *Appetite for America*, 377–78.

26. Porterfield, *Dining by Rail*, 109.

27. Frattasio, *Dining on the Shore Line Route*, 36.

28. Grant, *Railroads and the American People*, 148.

29. Ibid., 71–72.

30. Grant, *We Took the Train*, 142.

Chapter 7

1. Karl Zimmerman, *20th Century Limited* (St. Paul, MN: MBI Publishing Company, 2002), 97.

2. "New Hopes & Ancient Rancors," *Time*, September 27, 1948, www.time.com (accessed November 12, 2013).

3. Zimmerman, *20th Century Limited*, 114–15.

4. Ibid., 116.

5. Jaroslav Pelikan, "Flying Is for the Birds," *Cresset*, Volume 21, Number 10 (October 1958), 6–9, www.thecresset.org (accessed November 12, 2013).

6. Marc Frattasio, *Dining on the Shore Line Route* (Lynchburg, VA: TLC Publishing, 2003), 50–55.

7. George O. Shields, *Recreation*, Volume 10 (1899).

8. 1966 Magazine Ad for Fernando Lamas Hawks Heublein Cocktails.

9. New Haven Railroad Historical and Technical Association, www.nhrhta.org (accessed October 17, 2013).

10. "Meal-A-Mat on Central Opens New Era," *Headlight*, Volume 24, Number 2 (October–November 1963), 5, http://www.canadasouthern.com/caso/headlight/images/headlight-1063 (accessed November 12, 2013).

11. Ed Ruffing, "Central Replaces Sterling with Nickel," *Utica Daily Press*, September 21, 1963, 1.

12. "Meal-A-Mat," Editorial, *Nunda News* (Nunda, Livingston County, New York), October 1963.

13. Thomas Rawlins, "Dining Cars: They're Going out of Style," *St. Petersburg Times*, October 27, 1963,

14. Zimmerman, *20th Century Limited*, 114.

15. Lucius Beebe, *Mansions on Rails: The Folklore of the Private Railway Car* (Berkeley, CA: Howell-North, 1959), 25, 361.

16. Virginia City Private Railcar History, http://www.vcrail.com/vchistory_railcars.htm (accessed November 12, 2013).

17. Beebe, *Mansions*, 211–12, 371.

18. Ian Fleming, *From Russia with Love* (New York City: MJF Books, 1993), 200–217.

19. "Europe: Off Goes the Orient Express," *Time*, October 31, 1960, www.time.com (accessed November 13, 2013).

20. "Travel: Luxury Abroad," *Time*, June 29, 1962. www.time.com(accessed November 13, 2013).

21. Joseph Wechsberg, "Take the Orient Express," *New Yorker*, April 22, 1950, 83–94, http://www.josephwechsberg.com/html/wechsberg-new_yorker-articles (accessed November 13, 2013).

22. Joseph Wechsberg, "Last Man on the Orient Express," *Saturday Review*, March 17, 1962, 53–55, http://www.unz.org/Pub/SaturdayRev-1962 (accessed November 13, 2013).

23. Pelikan, "Flying Is for the Birds."

24. Wolfgang Schivelbusch, *The Railway Journey: The Industrialization of Time and Space in the 19th Century* (Berkeley: University of California Press, 1986), 12–14.

25. Railroad Museums Worldwide, www.railmuseums.com (accessed November 13, 2013).

26. Sacramento History Online, www.sacramentohistory.org, (accessed November 13, 2013).

27. Napa Valley Wine Train, www.winetrain.com (accessed November 13, 2013).

28. The Ice Cream Train, www.newportdinnertrain.com (accessed November 13, 2013).

29. Railroad Museum of Pennsylvania, www.rrmuseumpa.org (accessed November 13, 2013).

30. Bluebell Railway, www.bluebell-railway.com/golden-arrow (accessed November 13, 2013).

31. The East Lancashire Railway, www.eastlancsrailway.org.uk (accessed November 13, 2013).

32. Wayne Drehs, "All Aboard! Gamecocks Tailgate in Style," www.espn.go.com (accessed November 13, 2013).

33. Katherine Shaver, "Private Rail Car Owners Enjoy Yacht on Tracks," *Washington Post*, September 1, 2011, http://www.washingtonpost.com (accessed November 13, 2013.

34. Train Chartering Rail Charters, Luxury & Private Train Hire, www.train chartering.com (accessed November 13, 2013).

35. Shirley Sherwood, *Venice Simplon Orient-Express: The Return of the World's Most Celebrated Train* (London: Weidenfeld & Nicolson, 1983), 9.

Bibliography

Books

Acworth, W.M. *The Railways of England* (London: John Murray, 1889).

Allen, Geoffrey Freeman. *Railways of the Twentieth Century* (New York: W.W. Norton, 1983).

Barsley, Michael. *The Orient Express: The Story of the World's Most Fabulous Train* (New York: Stein and Day, 1967).

Beebe, Lucius. *Mansions on Rails: The Folklore of the Private Railway Car* (Berkeley, CA: Howell-North, 1959).

———. *20th Century: The Greatest Train in the World* (Berkeley, CA: Howell-North, 1962).

Beebe, Lucius Morris. *High Iron: A Book of Trains* (New York: D. Appleton-Century Co., 1938).

———. *Mr. Pullman's Elegant Palace Car* (New York: Doubleday, 1961).

Beebe, Lucius Morris, and Charles Clegg. *Hear the Train Blow: A Pictorial Epic of America in the Railroad Age* (New York: Dutton, 1952).

———. *The Age of Steam: A Classic Album of American Railroading* (New York: Rinehart, 1957).

———. *The Trains We Rode* (Berkeley, CA: Howell-North Books, 1965–1966).

Behrend, George. *Luxury Trains from the Orient Express to the TGV* (New York: Vendome Press, 1982).

Boddam-Whetham, & John Whetham. *Western Wanderings: A Record of Travel in the Evening Land* (London: Spottiswoode and Co., 1874).

Burton, Anthony. *The Orient Express: The History of the Orient Express Service from 1883 to 1950* (Edison, NJ: Chartwell Books, 2001).

Burton, David. *The Raj at Table* (London: Faber and Faber, 1994).

Carlin, Joseph M. *Cocktails: A Global History* (London: Reaktion Books, 2012).

Chevalier, Michel. *Society, Manners, and Politics in the United States*. Edited and with an Introduction by John William Ward (Ithaca, NY: Cornell University Press, 1961). Originally published in 1840.

Christie, Agatha. *Murder on the Orient Express* (Toronto: Bantam Books, 1983).

Clark, Francis E. *The Great Siberian Railway: What I Saw on My Journey* (London: S.W. Partridge and Co., 1904).

Colquhoun, Kate. *Murder in the First-Class Carriage* (New York: Overlook Press, 2011).

Cookridge, E.H. *Orient Express: The Life and Times of the World's Most Famous Train* (New York: Random House, 1978).

Coward, Noel. *Quadrille: A Romantic Comedy in Three Acts* (New York: Doubleday, 1955).

Denby, Elaine. *Grand Hotels* (London: Reaktion Books, 1998).

Dickens, Charles. *The Uncommercial Traveller* (New York: President Publishing Company, n.d.).

Drabble, Dennis. *The Great American Railroad War* (New York: St. Martin's Press, 2012).

Edmunds, Lowell. *Martini, Straight Up: The Classic American Cocktail* (Baltimore: Johns Hopkins University Press, 1998).

Fleming, Ian. *From Russia with Love* (New York: MJF Books, 1993).

Foster, George. *The Harvey House Cookbook: Memories of Dining along the Santa Fe Railroad* (Atlanta: Longstreet Press, 1992).

Frattasio, Marc. *Dining on the Shore Line Route: The History and Recipes of the New Haven Railroad Dining Car Department* (Lynchburg, VA: TLC Publishing, 2003).

Fried, Stephen. *Appetite for America: How Visionary Businessman Fred Harvey Built a Railroad Hospitality Empire That Civilized the Wild West* (New York: Bantam Books, 2010).

Goodman, Matthew. *Eighty Days: Nellie Bly and Elizabeth Bisland's History-Making Race Around the World* (New York: Ballantine Books, 2013).

Grant, H. Roger. *We Took the Train* (DeKalb: Northern Illinois University Press, 1990).

———. *Railroads and the American People* (Bloomington: Indiana University Press, 2012).

Greco, Thomas. *Dining on the B&O: Recipes and Sidelights from a Bygone Age.* (Baltimore: Johns Hopkins University Press, 2009).

Greene, Graham. *Stamboul Train* (New York: Penguin Books, 1932).

Haber, Barbara. *From Hardtack to Home Fries: An Uncommon History of American Cooks and Meals* (New York: Free Press, 2002).

Hamilton, Michael. *Down Memory Line* (Leitrim, Ireland: Drumlin, 1997).

Harper, Hill. *The Wealth Cure: Putting Money in Its Place* (New York: Penguin Group, 2012).

Hebron, Chris de Winter. *Dining at Speed: A Celebration of 125 Years of Railway Catering* (Kettering: Silver Link, 2004).

Herlihy, Patricia. *Vodka: A Global History* (London: Reaktion Books, 2012).

Hollister, Will C. *Dinner in the Diner: Great Railroad Recipes of All Time* (Los Angeles: Trans-Anglo Books, 1967).

Hudson, T.S. *A Scamper Through America or, Fifteen Thousand Miles of Ocean and Continent in Sixty Days* (London: Griffith & Farran, 1882).

Husband, Joseph. *The Story of the Pullman Car* (Chicago: A.C. McClurg & Co., 1917).

James, Henry. *The American Scene* (New York: Harper & Brothers, 1907).

Kalla-Bishop, Peter M., and John W. Wood. *The Golden Years of Trains: 1830–1920* (New York: Crescent Books, in association with Phoebus, 1977).

Katz, Solomon, ed. *Encyclopedia of Food and Culture* (New York: Charles Scribner's Sons, 2003).

Kerr, Michael, ed. *Last Call for the Dining Car: The Telegraph Book of Great Railway Journeys* (London: Aurum, 2009).

King, Moses. *King's Handbook of New York City: An Outline History and Description of the American Metropolis* (Boston: Moses King, 1892).

Kornweibel, Theodore. *Railroads in the African American Experience: A Photographic Journey* (Baltimore: Johns Hopkins University Press, 2010).

Lang, Jenifer Harvey, ed. *Larousse Gastronomique* (New York: Crown Publishers, 1990).

Levenstein, Harvey, *Revolution at the Table: The Transformation of the American Diet* (New York: Oxford University Press, 1988).

———. *Paradox of Plenty: A Social History of Eating in Modern America* (New York: Oxford University Press, 1993).

Leyendecker, Liston Edgington. *Palace Car Prince: A Biography of George Mortimer Pullman* (Niwot: University Press of Colorado, 1992).

Lovegrove, Keith. *Railroad: Identity, Design and Culture* (New York: Rizzoli, 2005).

Loveland, Jim. *Dinner Is Served: Fine Dining Aboard the Southern Pacific* (San Marino, CA: Golden West Books, 1996).

Macaulay, James. *Across the Ferry: First Impressions of America and Its People* (London: Hodder and Stoughton, 1884).

Marshall, James. *Santa Fe: The Railroad That Built an Empire* (New York: Random House, 1945).

Martin, Albro. *Railroads Triumphant: The Growth, Rejection, and Rebirth of a Vital American Force* (New York: Oxford University Press, 1992).

Marryat, Frederick. *A Diary in America, with Remarks on Its Institutions.* Edited with notes and an introduction by Sydney Jackman (New York: Alfred A. Knopf, 1962). Originally published in 1839.

McKenzie, William A. *Dining Car Line to the Pacific* (St. Paul: Minnesota Historical Society Press, 1990).

Mencken, August. *The Railroad Passenger Car* (Baltimore and London: Johns Hopkins University Press, 2000).

Moerlein, George. *A Trip Around the World* (Cincinnati: M&R Burgheim, 1886).

Monkswell, Robert Alfred Hardcastle Collier. *French Railways* (London: Smith, Elder & Co., 1911).

Murray, John. *Murray's Handbook to London as It Is* (London: J. Murray, 1879).

Nichols, Beverley. *No Place Like Home* (London: Jonathan Cape Ltd., 1936).

Pennsylvania Railroad. *The Pennsylvania Railroad Dining Car Department, Instructions.* (Philadelphia: Pennsylvania Railroad, Dining Car Department, 1938).

Pham, John-Peter. *Heirs of the Fisherman: Behind the Scenes of Papal Death and Succession* (London: Oxford University Press, 2006).

Poling-Kempes, Lesley. *The Harvey Girls: Women Who Opened the West* (New York: Paragon House, 1989).

Porterfield, James D. *Dining by Rail: The History and Recipes of America's Golden Age of Railroad Cuisine* (New York: St. Martin's Press, 1993).

Rae, W.F. *Westward by Rail: The New Route to the East* (London: Longmans, Green, and Co., 1870).

Schivelbusch, Wolfgang. *The Railway Journey: The Industrialization of Time and Space in the 19th Century* (Berkeley: University of California Press, 1986).

Shaw, Timothy. *The World of Escoffier* (New York: Vendome Press, 1995).

Sherwood, Shirley. *Venice Simplon Orient-Express: The Return of the World's Most Celebrated Train* (London: Weidenfeld & Nicolson, 1983).

Simmons, Jack. *The Victorian Railway* (London: Thames and Hudson, 1991).

Smith, Andrew. *American Tuna: The Rise and Fall of an Improbable Food* (Berkeley: University of California Press, 2012).

Smith, Andrew, ed. *The Oxford Encyclopedia of Food and Drink in America* (New York: Oxford University Press, 2004).

Société nationale des chemins de fer français. *Les Plats régionaux des buffets gastronomiques.* Introduction by Curnonsky (Paris: Chaix, 1951).

Thomas, Jerry. *How to Mix Drinks, or The Bon-Vivant's Companion* (New York: Dick & Fitzgerald, 1862).

Trollope, Anthony. *He Knew He Was Right* (London: Penguin Books, 1994).

Unwin, Philip. *Travelling by Train in the Edwardian Age* (London: George Allen & Unwin, 1979).

White, John H. Jr. *The American Railroad Passenger Car* (Baltimore: Johns Hopkins University Press, 1978).

Withey, Lynne. *Grand Tours and Cook's Tours: A History of Leisure Travel, 1750–1915* (New York: William Morrow and Company, 1997).

Wolmar, Christian. *Blood, Iron, and Gold* (New York: Public Affairs, 2010).

Zimmerman, Karl. *20th Century Limited* (St. Paul, MN: MBI Publishing Company, 2002).

Periodicals

Nunda News, "Meal-A-Mat," Nunda, Livingston County, New York. Thursday, October, 1963.

Rawlins, Thomas. "Dining Cars: They're Going out of Style." *St. Petersburg Times*, October 27, 1963.

Recreation Magazine, Volume 10, 1899 (New York: G.O. Shields, 1899).

Ruffing, Ed. "Central Replaces Sterling with Nickel." *Utica Daily Press*, Saturday, September 21, 1963.

Wechsberg, Joseph. "The World of Wagon-Lits." *Gourmet*, June 1970.

———. "The Great Blue Train." *Gourmet*, March 1971.

Websites

Ad. 1966. Fernando Lamas Hawks Heublein Cocktails. www.ebay.com. Accessed December 10, 2013.

The American Magazine. Volume 85, 1918, 144. www.babel.hathatrust.org. Accessed April 14, 2013.

American Southwestern Railway Association, Inc. "Little Nugget." http://www .mcscom.com/asra/nugget.htm. Accessed September 26, 2013.

Beebe, Lucius. "Purveyor to the West." *American Heritage Magazine* 18, no. 2 (February 1967). http://www.americanheritage.com. Accessed May 6, 2013.

Bluebell Railway. www.bluebell-railway.com/golden-arrow. Accessed November 13, 2013.

Browne, Malcolm W. "The 20th Century Makes Final Run." *The New York Times*, December 3, 1967. www.nytimes.com archive. Accessed September 19, 2013.

Central Pacific Railroad Photographic History Museum. "Across the Continent. From the Missouri to the Pacific Ocean by Rail." *The New York Times*, June 28, 1869. www.cprr.org. Accessed April 10, 2013.

Cook, Thomas. *Cook's Excursionist*, August 28, 1863. In *Oxford Dictionary of National Biography*, 2013. www.oup.com/oxforddnb/info. Accessed April 5, 2013.

Denver Post. "Streamliner Train: City of Denver." http://blogs.denverpost.com/ library/2013/06/12/union-pacifics-city-of-denver-streamliner-train/8643/. Accessed September 26, 2013.

Dictionary of Victorian London. www.victorianlondon.org. Accessed May 21, 2013.

Drehs, Wayne. "All Aboard! Gamecocks Tailgate in Style." www.espn.go.com. Accessed November 13, 2013.

The East Lancashire Railway. www.eastlancsrailway.org.uk. Accessed November 13, 2013.

Estes, Rufus. *Good Things to Eat, As Suggested by Rufus* (Chicago: The Author, c. 1911). Feeding America. http://digital.lib.mus.edu. Accessed August 6, 2013.

Grace, Michael L. "The Twentieth Century Limited." http://www.newyorksocialdiary .com. Accessed September 10, 2013.

Headlight. "Meal-A-Mat on Central Opens New Era," 24, no. 2 (October–November 1963). http://www.canadasouthern.com/caso/headlight/images/headlight-1063 .pdf. Accessed April 8, 2014.

The Ice Cream Train. www.newportdinnertrain.com. Accessed November 13, 2013.

Janin, Jules. *The American in Paris* (Paris: Longman, Brown, Green, and Longmans, 1843). www.books.google.com. Accessed April 25, 2013.

Kinsella, Lucy. "Chicago Stories: Pullman Porters: From Servitude to Civil Rights." Window to the World Communications. www.wttw.com. Accessed April 10, 2013.

MacKay, Charles. *Life and Liberty on America: Sketches of a Tour in the United States and Canada in 1857–1958* (London: Smith, Elder and Co., 1859). www.books. google.com. Accessed April 5, 2013.

Morris, Gay. "Dance: 'Le Train Bleu' Makes a Brief Stopover." *The New York Times,* March 4, 1990. http://www.nytimes.com/1990/03/04/arts. Accessed August 9, 2013.

Mulligan, Terence. "The Delights of Pullman Dining USA, 1866–1968." Pullman Car Services Supplement Edition, April 2007. www.semgonline.com. Accessed April 9, 2013.

Napa Valley Wine Train. www.winetrain.com. Accessed November 13, 2013.

National Institute on Alcohol Abuse and Alcoholism. "3.2% Beer." http://alcohol policy.niaaa.nih.gov/3_2_beer_2.html. Accessed September 25, 2013.

New Haven Railroad Historical and Technical Association. www.nhrhta.org. Accessed October 17, 2013.

New York Public Library Menu Collection. http://menus.nypl.org/menu. Accessed April 24, 2013.

The New York Times. "Paderewski Chef Quits Pullman Job." January 3, 1928. www .nytimes.com. Accessed April 10, 2013.

———. "Pullman Dining Cars: A Trial Trip on the English Midland Railway." From the *London News,* July 8. July 19, 1882. www.query.nytimes.com. Accessed May 21, 2013.

———. "Spies on Pullman Cars." February 6, 1886. www.nytimes.com. Accessed April 10, 2013.

Pelikan, Jaroslav. "Flying Is for the Birds." *The Cresset* 21, no. 10 (October 1958): 6–9. www.thecresset.org. Accessed November 12, 2013.

Pullman State Historic Site. www.pullman-museum.org. Accessed March 26, 2013.

Railroad Museum of Pennsylvania. www.rrmuseumpa.org. Accessed November 13, 2013.

Railroad Museums Worldwide. www.railmuseums.com. Accessed November 13, 2013.

Railway Age. February 16, 1924, 76–77. www.foodtimeline.org/restaurants.html #childmenus. Accessed August 15, 2013.

Railway Gazette. December 9, 1887, 796. http://www.books.google.com. Accessed August 12, 2013.

Railway Magazine. December 1897. "To Sunny Italy by the Rome Express: An Account of the First Journey by a Passenger." http://books.google.com. Accessed May 20, 1013.

Sacramento History Online. "*Southern Pacific Bulletin*." www.sacramentohistory.org. Accessed September 17, 2013.

Sekon, G.A., ed. *Railway Magazine* 7 (July–December, 1900): 520–521. http://books .google.com. Accessed August 9, 2013.

Shaver, Katherine. "Private Rail Car Owners Enjoy Yacht on Tracks." *Washington Post*, September 1, 2011. http://www.washingtonpost.com. Accessed November 13, 2013.

T.F.R. *Railway Magazine*. "The Pleasures of the Dining-Car," Vol. 7 (July–December, 1900): 520–521. http://books.google.com. Accessed May 21, 2013.

Time. "Europe: Off Goes the Orient Express." October 31, 1960. www.time.com. Accessed May 21, 2013.

———. "Foreign News: Orient Express." April 29, 1935. www.time.com. Accessed September 10, 2013.

———. "New Hopes & Ancient Rancors." September 27, 1948. www.time.com. Accessed November 12, 2013.

———. "Travel: Luxury Abroad." June 29, 1962. www.time.com. Accessed November 13, 2013.

Train Chartering Rail Charters. Luxury and private train hire. www.trainchartering .com. Accessed November 13, 2013.

United States Patent Office. Patent No. 89,537, April 27, 1869. www.uspto.gov. Accessed April 10, 2013.

University of Nevada, Las Vegas. http://digital.library.univ.edu/objects/menus. Accessed January 29, 2013.

Virginia City Private Railcar History. http://www.vcrail.com/vchistory_railcars.htm. Accessed November 12, 2013.

Wechsberg, Joseph. "Last Man on the Orient Express." *The Saturday Review*, March 17, 1962, 53–55. http://www.unz.org/Pub/SaturdayRev-1962. Accessed November 13, 2013.

———. "Take the Orient Express," *The New Yorker*, April 22, 1950, 83–94. http:// www.josephwechsberg.com/html/wechsberg-new_yorker-articles. Accessed November 13, 2013.

Western Pacific Railroad Dining Car Menu [19--]. California State Railroad Museum Library. www.sacramentohistory.org. Accessed September 26, 2013.

Index

Numbers in *italics* refer to illustrations; numbers in **bold,** to recipes.

About the Author

Jeri Quinzio is the author of *Pudding: A Global History* and *Of Sugar and Snow: A History of Ice Cream Making*, which won the International Association of Culinary Professionals Culinary History Award in 2010. She is an area editor and contributor to *The Oxford Companion to Sweets*, and has contributed to works including *The Oxford Encyclopedia of Food and Drink in America* and *Culinary Biographies*. She is also a board member of the Culinary Historians of Boston.